*graphic designers
in europe/1*

graphic designers

in europe/1

Jan Lenica
Jean-Michel Folon
Josef Müller-Brockmann
Dick Elffers

Universe Books ✳ *New York*

Edited by Henri Hillebrand
Original texts by the artists
English translation by Jeanpierre Bendel
Design by Gan Hosoya

Published in the United States of America
in 1971 by Universe Books
381 Park Avenue South
New York, N.Y. 10016

Library of Congress Catalog Card
Number: 72-147894
ISBN 0-87663-143-X
Printed and bound in Japan

Table des matières
Table of contents
Inhaltsverzeichnis

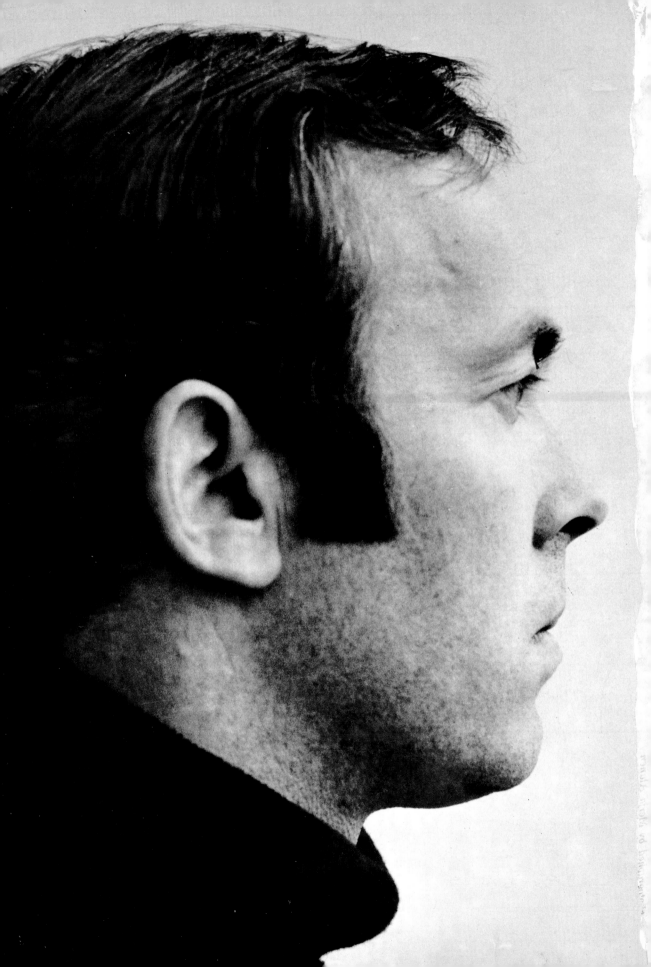

Lenica

Jan Lenica

L'un des charmes de l'affiche est dû au hasard qui préside à son apparition. Je ne sais jamais en quel lieu et dans quel cadre je rencontrerai mon affiche (sur une palissade entourant une maison en construction, ou sur le mur d'une chaumière, au milieu des poules et des oies), par quel temps, à quelle heure et quelle sera mon humeur. Le voisinage imprévisible d'autres affiches crée parfois des contrastes surprenants, des significations inattendues. Dans une exposition ou dans une galerie, l'affiche est dépouillée de ces charmes.

Je n'ai encore rencontré personne qui soit allé au cinéma, incité à voir un film par l'affiche qui l'annonçait. C'est pourquoi il est absurde d'exiger de l'affiche de cinéma qu'elle remplisse la caisse; ce sont des facteurs tout à fait différents qui sont déterminants, tels que le nom des acteurs, parfois la personnalité du metteur en scène, l'opinion publique, le fait qu'un roman célèbre ait été adapté à l'écran, etc. Cela ne veut pas dire que l'affiche de cinéma ne soit pas nécessaire; tout simplement, il ne faut pas exiger d'elle des choses

One of the charming things about posters is the element of chance governing their appearance. I never know where I am going to come upon one of my posters or what the surroundings will be (a hoarding around a building site or the wall of a thatched cottage among the chickens and geese), what the wheather will be like, what time of the day it will be, and what sort of temper I shall be in. The unforeseeable juxtaposition of other posters sometimes creates astonishing contrasts and unexpected meaning. Exhibited at a show or in a gallery, a poster loses this particular charm.

I have never met anyone who went to the cinema to see a film because the poster announcing it had induced him to do so. For this reason, it is absurd to expect a cinema poster to fill the till; what determines financial success are quite different factors, such as the names of the stars, perhaps the personality of the director, public opinion, the fact that a famous novel has been adapted for the screen and the like. This is not to say that cinema posters are not necessary, but

Was Plakate so reizvoll macht, ist nicht zuletzt der Zufall, der ihr Erscheinen bestimmt. Ich weiß nie, wo und in welcher Umgebung einer Bretterwand, die einen Bauplatz umgrenzt, oder an der Außenwand einer Scheune (inmitten einer Schar Hühner oder Gänse), bei welchem Wetter, zu welcher Zeit und in welcher Stimmung ich meinem Plakat begegnen werde.

Auch die nicht voraussehbare Nachbarschaft zu anderen Plakaten ergibt oft überraschende Kontraste, einen unerwarteten Sinn. In einer Ausstellung oder Galerie wird das Plakat seines spezifischen Reizes beraubt.

Ich habe noch niemanden getroffen, der auf ein Filmplakat hin ins Kino ging. Es ist deshalb absurd, von einem Filmplakat zu verlangen, daß es die Kassen füllt. Es sind ganz andere Faktoren, die hier den Ausschlag geben: die Namen der Darsteller, die Persönlichkeit des Regisseurs, die öffentliche Meinung, die Tatsache, daß ein bekannter Roman verfilmt wurde, usw. Was nicht heißen soll, das Kinoplakat sei überflüssig: man darf von ihm ganz einfach nichts Un-

7

Jan Lenica

impossibles. L'affiche ne fait qu'annoncer le film, elle informe de son caractère et de son climat; elle est le raccourci visuel du film. Son propos est fait de probité dans l'information, même si la liberté d'interprétation plastique est poussée à l'extrême. On ne saurait exiger de l'affiche qu'elle mente, ou qu'elle promette quelque chose qui n'est pas dans le film.

La ressemblance tue l'affiche. D'où le danger d'une manière, d'un style adopté par tout le monde: une affiche semblable aux autres meurt dans la rue. Désireux de voir mon affiche efficiente, je dois parfois rompre mon propre style, modifier ma manière. J'ai recours à des moyens radicalement différents, je change d'instrument de travail, je cherche une technique

me permettant d'attaquer différemment la surface blanche du papier. Lorsque je fus, il y a quelque temps, frappé par la tendance à rendre la composition plus touffue et à la surcharger de détails, j'ai fait une affiche vide.

Qui suis-je? Je n'ai jamais été capable de remplir de façon satisfaisante les questionnaires officiels. «Designer»? Ce terme a un relent de bureau et, de plus, on ne sait pas au juste ce qu'il signifie. D'ailleurs, je ne me contente pas de dessiner des affiches, je fais également des films. «Directeur de film»? En réalité, je ne suis pas un

simply that the impossible should not be expected of them. The poster does no more than announce the film and provide information about its type and climate—it is a visual summary of the film. It is tied to accuracy of information even though the flexibility in freedom of expression is pushed to the extreme. No one can expect a poster to tell lies or to promise something that the film does not contain.

Similarity is the death of posters. This means that there is danger in mannerisms or in a style that everyone can copy. A poster that looks like other posters is a dead loss in the street. As I like to feel that my posters do a job, I sometimes have to break out of my own style and modify my mannerisms. I make use of radically different techniques, change my working instruments, seek techniques that allow me to attack the virgin surface of the paper in a different way. When, some time ago, I noted a tendency to cram too much into the composition and to overload the details, I did a poster with nothing in it.

If you want to know who I am, I am a person who has never been able to provide satisfactorily the information about "occupation" demanded by official questionnaires. "Designer"? This is a term that smacks of the office and nobody really knows what it means. Besides, I do not confine myself to designing posters, I make films, too. "Film director"? To be quite accurate, I do not just handle the direction, I make my films all by myself, I write the scenarios, design them, do the animation, and carry out the cutting. I operate around the boundaries of the visual arts, films, and literature, and there is no word in the dictionaries for activities of this kind.

In present-day society, art is reserved for a select minority. For this reason, the thing that has always attracted me most about

mögliches verlangen. Das Plakat kann nicht mehr tun als ankündigen und über dessen Charakter und Atmosphäre informieren. Es stellt so etwas wie einen visuellen Abriß des Films dar. Sein Zweck ist die zuverlässige Übermittlung von Information, auch wenn die Freiheit der Darstellung bis zum Äußersten getrieben wird. Man kann vom Plakat nicht verlangen, daß es lügt oder etwas verspricht, was im Film nicht enthalten ist.

Ähnlichkeit ist tödlich für das Plakat. Hier liegen die Gefahren einer Manier, eines Stils, den jeder kopieren kann. Ein Plakat, das aussieht, wie andere Plakate, wird auf der Straße nicht gesehen, weil es nicht «da» ist. Wenn mir daran liegt, daß mein Plakat wirksam ist, muß ich zuweilen meinen eigenen Stil wechseln, meine Ausdrucksweise ändern. Ich greife zu völlig anderen Methoden, ich nehme ganz neue Arbeitsgeräte zu Hilfe, ich suche eine Technik, die mir erlaubt, mich auf andere Art an die weiße Fläche des Papiers heranzuwagen. Als ich vor einiger Zeit eine Neigung bei mir bemerkte, die Komposition mit Einzelheiten zu überladen, entwarf ich ein leeres Plakat.

Wer ich bin? Ich bin nie fähig gewesen, in den amtlichen Formularen die Frage nach dem Beruf zufriedenstellend zu beantworten. «Designer»? Dieses Wort riecht nach Büro, zudem weiß man nicht genau, was es bedeutet. Übrigens begnüge ich mich nicht damit, Plakate zu entwerfen, ich mache auch Filme. Also «Filmregisseur»? Aber ich habe nie Regie geführt. Ich mache meine Filme ganz allein. Ich schreibe das Drehbuch, entwerfe die Figuren und Kulissen, fertige die Phasen an und besorge den Schnitt. Ich arbeite in den Bereichen der visuellen Kunst, des Films und der Literatur zugleich. Aber in keinem Lexikon findet sich ein Ausdruck, der eine solche Tätigkeit bezeichnet. In der heutigen Gesellschaft ist die Kunst der Elite vorbehalten. Aus diesem Grunde

Jan Lenica

metteur en scène, je fais mes films à moi tout seul, j'en écris le scénario, je les dessine, je les anime et j'en fais le montage. J'évolue aux confins des arts plastiques, du film et de la littérature; or, pour pareille activité, il n'y a aucun terme dans les dictionnaires.

Dans la société actuelle, l'art est réservé à une élite. C'est pourquoi, ce qui m'a toujours le plus attiré, est ce qui est en marge de l'art: ses formes populaires, ce qui s'adresse aux masses, soit l'art primitif de la civilisation contemporaine. Avec l'aide de ces «mass-media», j'essaye de faire passer mes idées en contrebande. Cette optique n'est pas nouvelle: Dostoïevski déjà habillait ses idées du manteau du roman policier.

Je reconnais qu'en faisant une affiche pour une pièce de théâtre ou un film, je m'intéresse souvent davantage à tout ce qui environne ces œuvres, plutôt qu'à elles-mêmes: dans quel milieu elles ont surgi, à quelle époque, quelles sont leurs affinités de style, leur rôle actuel. Pour moi, rendre sensible mon attitude envers l'œuvre est aussi important, sinon plus, qu'exprimer la pensée de l'auteur. Je ne suis pas en mesure d'adopter une attitude objective à l'égard d'un drame qui est éventé depuis longtemps et n'émeut plus personne aujourd'hui. C'est pourquoi mon affiche pour le «Faust» de Gounod n'est pas tout à fait sérieuse: c'est un Faust inspiré par les démons parisiens du siècle dernier, un Goethe aux Folies-Bergères, un diable jaillissant d'une bouche de métro.

Lorsque je travaillais à l'affiche d'«Alexandre Newski», le film d'Eisenstein, je pensais sans discontinuer au pathétique épique de ce film; mais lorsque je montrai cette maquette à quelqu'un, je vis un sourire sur son visage. Je fus tout d'abord surpris par cette réaction inattendue, car dans ce film il n'y a rien de risible: on y torture, on y jette des enfants dans les

art is its fringe, its popular forms, whatever it aimed at the masses— in other words, the primitive art of contemporary civilization. Using these mass media, I try to smuggle my ideas across. This is not a new point of view: Dostoievsky for example cloaked his ideas in detective novels.

I realize that by making a poster for a play or a film I am generally more interested in everything around the work than in the work itself— the circumstances and age from which it has been taken, their stylistic relationships, their role at the present time. For me, expressing my attitude to the work is as important, if not more so, as expressing the ideas of the author. I am not capable of taking an objective attitude to a drama that was out of date long ago and has no emotional appeal for anyone today. That is why my poster for Gounod's "Faust" is not entirely serious. This is a Faust inspired by the Parisian demons of the last century, Goethe at the Folies-Bergères, a devil springing up out of a metro station.

When I was working on the poster for "Alexander Nevsky", the Eisenstein film, I kept trying to think about the epic pathos of the film, but when I showed the draft to someone I saw his smile. To start with I was surprised by this unexpected reaction, for there is nothing to laugh about in this film, only torture and throwing children into the fire. But after thinking it over

spielt sich das, was mich an der Kunst am meisten anzog, in ihren Grenzbezirken ab, in ihren volkstümlichen Formen, jenen Formen, welche die Massen ansprechen, oder in der primitiven Kunst der zeitgenössischen Zivilisation. Mit Hilfe dieser Massenmedien versuche ich meine Ideen in die Öffentlichkeit zu schmuggeln. Das ist nichts Neues. Schon Dostojewski kleidete seine Ideen in den Mantel des Kriminalromans.

Ich gebe zu, daß ich mich beim Entwerfen eines Film- oder Theaterplakats häufig für alles, was mit dem betreffenden Streifen oder Stück zusammenhängt, mehr, als für das Werk selbst interessiere. In welchem Milieu und zu welcher Zeit es entstand, worin die Feinheiten seines Stils bestehen, und was seine aktuelle Bedeutung ausmacht. Für mich ist es ebenso wichtig, wenn nicht wichtiger, meine Einstellung zum Werk sichtbar zu machen, als die Idee des Autors zum Ausdruck zu bringen. Ich bin nicht imstande, eine objektive Einstellung zu einem Drama zu haben, das vor langer Zeit geschrieben wurde und heute niemanden mehr bewegt. Deshalb ist mein Plakat für Gounods «Faust» nicht ganz ernst zu nehmen. Es ist ein von den Pariser Dämonen des letzten Jahrhunderts inspirierter Faust, ein Goethe der «Folies-Bergères», ein Teufel, der aus einem Ausgang der «Métro» heraushüpft. Als ich am Plakat für Eisensteins Film «Alexander Newski» arbeitete, dachte ich ununterbrochen an das epische Pathos dieses Films; aber als ich jemandem die Skizze zeigte, lächelte der. Ich war von dieser Reaktion zunächst überrascht, denn in dem Film gibt es nichts, das zum Lachen wäre: Man foltert, man wirft kleine Kinder in die Flammen. Nach einigem Nachdenken ließ ich den Entwurf dennoch unverändert. Der Film erzählt eine volkstümliche Legende. Eisenstein hatte die Grausamkeit der makabren Szenen, nach Art der Bilderbogen

Jan Lenica

flammes. Après réflexion, je laissai toutefois mon projet tel quel. Ce film est un conte populaire; à l'instar des images d'Epinal, Eisenstein, en les stylisant, avait atténué la cruauté des scènes macabres. Le caractère étranger de mon affiche, par rapport au film, provoque une surprise; son identification apparemment lointaine rejoint un autre aspect de l'œuvre.

Plus que la peinture, la littérature et le théâtre ont influencé le développement du cinéma. Les dessins animés, en vérité, ne sont faits que pour les enfants; parfois ils distraient les adultes, à l'égal d'un jouet. Et pourtant, c'est l'unique forme qui assure au cinéma le caractère d'œuvre d'art. La seule qui permette d'être créateur du commencement à la fin d'un film qui, de ce fait, perd tout caractère de produit collectif.

I left my draft as it was. This film is a popular legend, and on the model of the Epinal pictures, Eisenstein watered down the cruelty in these macabre scenes by stylizing them. The character of my poster gave rise to surprise because it was out of rapport with the film; the apparent lack of direct identification came from its orientation toward another aspect of the work.

Literature and the theater have influenced the development of the cinema much more than paintings. To be quite frank, animated drawings are made for children but sometimes amuse adults as well, just as a toy does. Yet this is the only form that ensures the production of a work of art in the cinema, the only one that permits creative artistry from the start of the film to its end by eliminating the aspect of the collective product.

von Epinal, durch Stilisierung gemindert. Der Charakter meines Plakats ruft Überraschung hervor, weil es nicht die übliche Beziehung zum Film aufweist. Die scheinbare Inkongruenz rührt davon her, daß sich das Plakat an einem anderen Aspekt des Films orientiert.

Mehr noch als von der Malerei wurde die Entwicklung der Filmkunst von der Literatur und vom Theater beeinflußt. Zeichentrickfilme sind eigentlich nur für Kinder gedacht; aber manchmal unterhalten sie den Erwachsenen ebenfalls, wie dies ja auch ein Spielzeug vermag, und dennoch ist es die einzige Form, die es einem erlaubt, vom Anfang bis zum Ende Schöpfer eines Films zu sein, sich eben dadurch von den Kollektiv-Erzeugnissen, die wir gemeinhin Film nennen, grundsätzlich unterscheidet.

Jan Lenica

de Vienne, Smyrne, Londres. Dessine deux stands pour le Salon de l'enfance à Paris.

1956 Illustre le livre d'enfant «Lokomotive», de Tuwin.

1957 Dessine son premier film d'animation «Il était une fois...».

1958 Edite une monographie de l'œuvre de Tadeusz Trepkowski, affichiste.

1959 Produit à Paris le film «Monsieur Tête».

1960 Expose ses affiches à Londres.

1962 Dessine avec Alfred Sauvy le livre «Population Explosion».

1963 Crée les décors, à l'opéra de Wiesbaden, pour l'opéra bouffe «Yolimba», de W. Killmayer.

1964 Réalise à Munich un film d'animation «Le Rhinocéros», d'après Ionesco.

1965 Expose ses travaux à la «Persona Exhibition» de Tokyo.

1966 Expose au Musée d'art cinématographique de Copenhague.

1967 Expose ses travaux graphiques à la «Visual Art Gallery» de New York.

1968 Expose à la Villa Stuck de Munich, et au Musée d'affiches de Varsovie.

1969 Termine un long métrage, film d'animation, «Adam 2». Tourne un court métrage, avec acteurs, «Still Life».

Nombreuses distinctions dans le domaine du film et de l'affiche: Lion d'argent (Venise), Grand Prix de la Foire internationale (Bruxelles), Prix de la critique (Tours), Prix Emile-Cohl (Paris), Premiers prix (Cracovie, Oberhausen), Prix de la critique polonaise du film, Dragon d'or (Cracovie), Prix officiel de la République fédérale d'Allemagne, Prix Toulouse-Lautrec (Paris), Premier et troisième prix (Karlovy-Vary), Premier prix (Varsovie).

Vienna, Izmir, and London. Designed two stands for the Salon de l'Enfance at Paris.

1956 Illustrated Tuwin's children's book "Lokomotive".

1957 Designed his first animated film "Once Upon a Time".

1958 Published a monograph on the work of Tadeusz Trepkowski, the poster artist.

1959 Produced the film "Monsieur Tête" in Paris.

1960 Exhibited his posters in London.

1962 Together with Alfred Sauvy designed the book "Population Explosion".

1963 Designed scenery for Wilhelm Killmayer's comic opera "Yolimba" for the Wiesbaden Opera.

1964 In Munich, created the animated film "The Rhinoceros", based on the Ionesco play.

1965 Exhibited his work at the Persona Exhibition in Tokyo.

1966 Exhibited at the Copenhagen Museum of Cinematographic Art.

1967 Exhibited his graphic work at the Visual Art Gallery, New York.

1968 Exhibited at the Villa Stuck, Munich, and at the Poster Museum, Warsaw.

1969 Completed a full-length animated film "Adam 2". Shot a short film (with actors) "Still Life".

Numerous distinctions in the fields of film and poster: Silver Lion (Venice), Grand Prix of the Brussels International Fair, Critics' Prize (Tours), Prix Emile-Cohl (Paris) first prizes (Krakow, Oberhausen), Golden Dragon (Polish critics' prize for films) (Krakow), official prize of the German Federal Republic, Prix Toulouse-Lautrec (Paris), first and third prizes (Karlovy-Vary), first prize (Warsaw).

1956 Illustriert Tuwins Kinderbuch «Lokomotive».

1957 Zeichnet seinen ersten Trickfilm «Es war einmal».

1958 Veröffentlicht eine Monographie über das Werk des Plakatmalers Tadeusz Trepkowski.

1959 Produktion des Films «Monsieur Tête» in Paris.

1960 Ausstellung seiner Plakate in London.

1962 Illustriert gemeinsam mit Alfred Sauvy das Buch «Population Explosion».

1963 Entwirft Bühnenbilder für die Aufführung der komischen Oper «Yolimba» von W. Killmayer in der Wiesbadener Oper.

1964 Zeichnet den Trickfilm «Das Rhinozeros» nach Ionesco.

1965 Mit eigenen Arbeiten in der «Persona Exhibition» in Tokio vertreten.

1966 Stellt im Museum für Filmkunst in Kopenhagen aus.

1967 Ausstellung seiner graphischen Arbeiten in der «Visual Art Gallery», New York.

1968 Ausstellung in der Villa Stuck in München und im Plakatmuseum in Warschau.

1969 Fertigstellung des abendfüllenden Trickfilms «Adam 2». Dreht mit Schauspielern den Kurzfilm «Still Life».

Viele Auszeichnungen auf dem Gebiet des Films und des Plakats. Silberner Löwe (Venedig); Großer Preis der Internationalen Messe (Brüssel); Kritiker-Preis (Tours), Emile-Cohl-Preis (Paris); Erster Preis (Krakau, Oberhausen); Polnischer Film-Preis, Golddrache (Krakau); Offizieller Preis der Bundesrepublik Deutschland; Toulouse-Lautrec-Preis (Paris); Erster und dritter Preis (Karlovy-Vary); Erster Preis (Warschau).

Jan Lenica

sezession

ALEXANDER NEWZKI

Atlas Film präsentiert: Alexander Newski
(UdSSR 1938)
Ein Film von S.M. Eisenstein
mit Nikolai Tscherkassow

Ein Exklusiv-Programm weltbekannter Filme.
Festival-Sieger, umstrittene Filme, berühmte
Außenseiter und klassische Meisterwerke werden
erstmals in deutschen Filmtheatern vorgestellt.

2

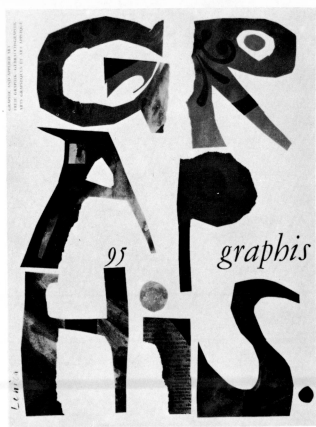

3

4

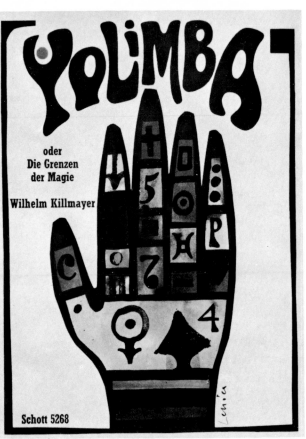

5

TEATR WIELKI
CHARLES GOUNOD
FAUST

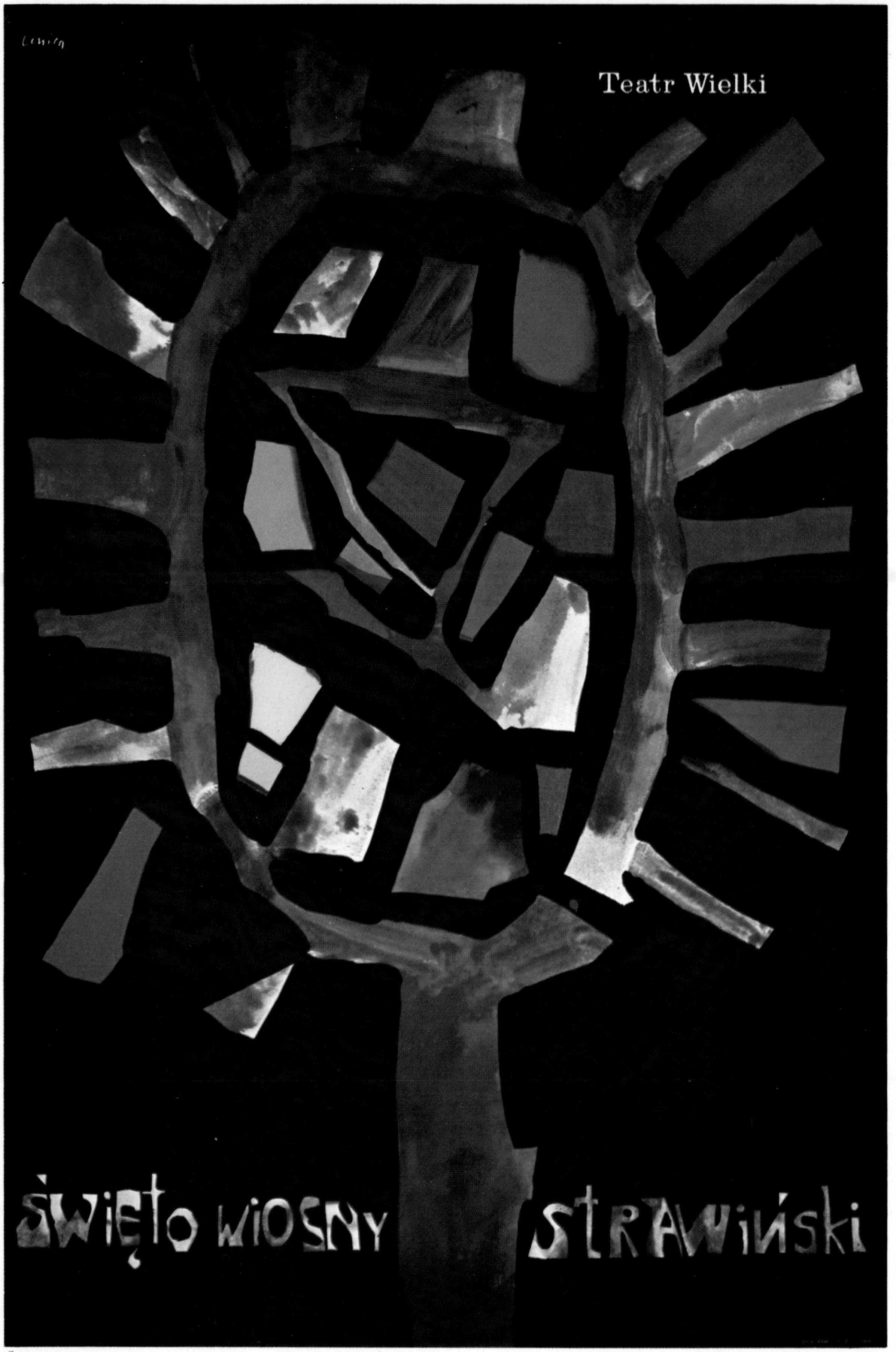

7

9

10

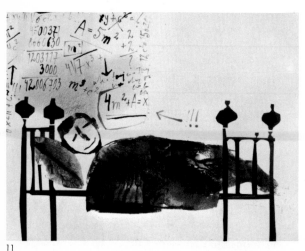

11

12

13

14

18

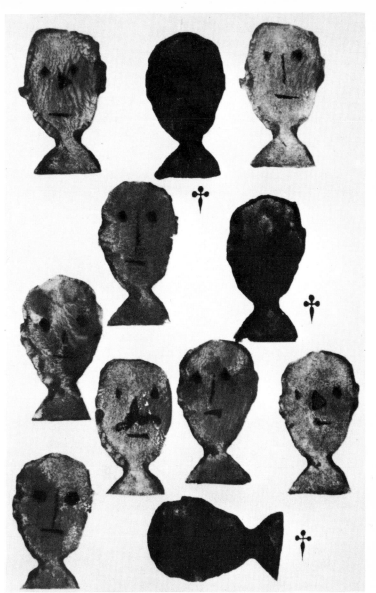

15

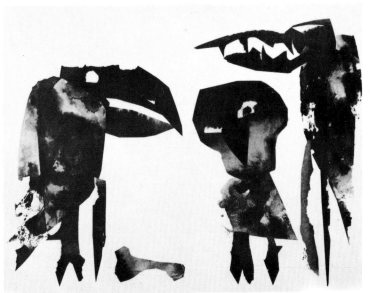

16

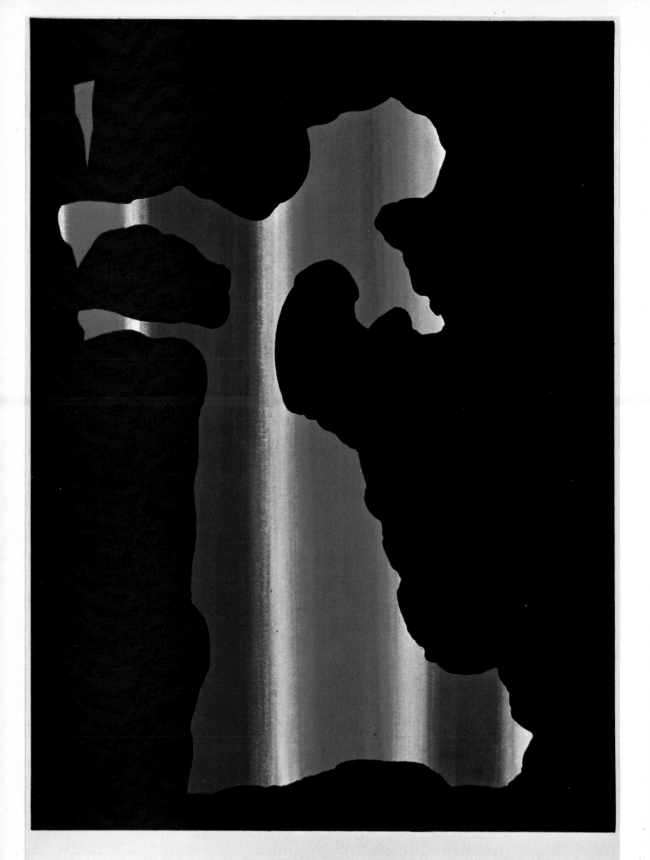

Richard Strauss ELEKTRA Teatr Wielki

TEATR NARODOWY w Warszawie 1957

Racine
FEDRA

19

20

21

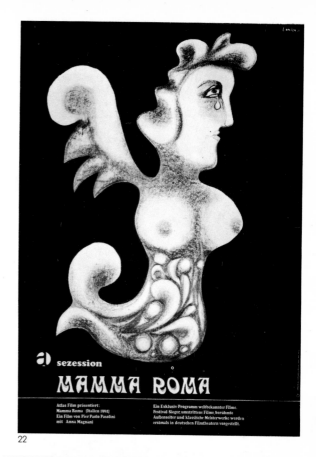

22

23

24

Teatr Wielki Otello Verdi

Teatr Wielki

BRITTEN **Wariacje na temat Purcella**

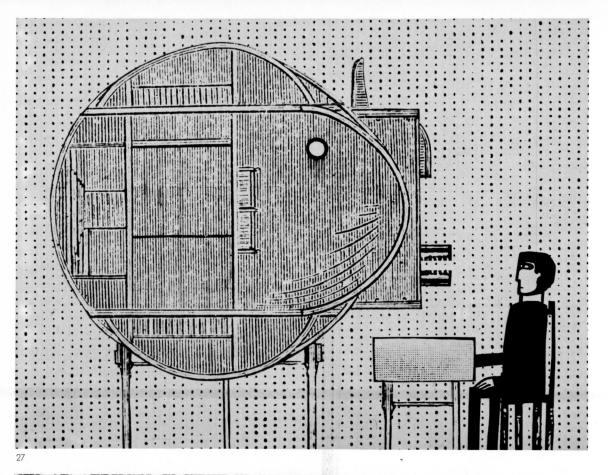

27

28

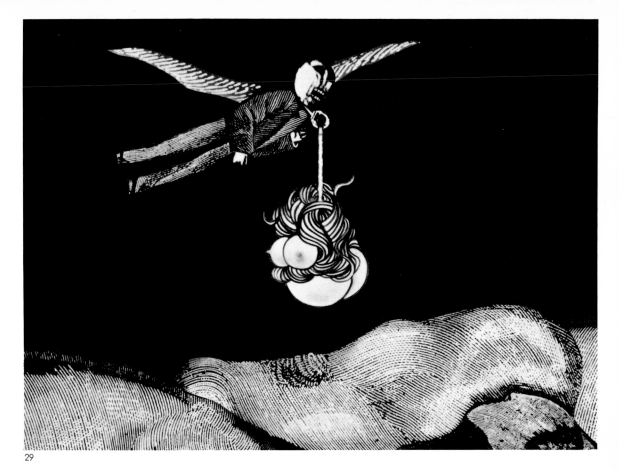

29

30

31

32

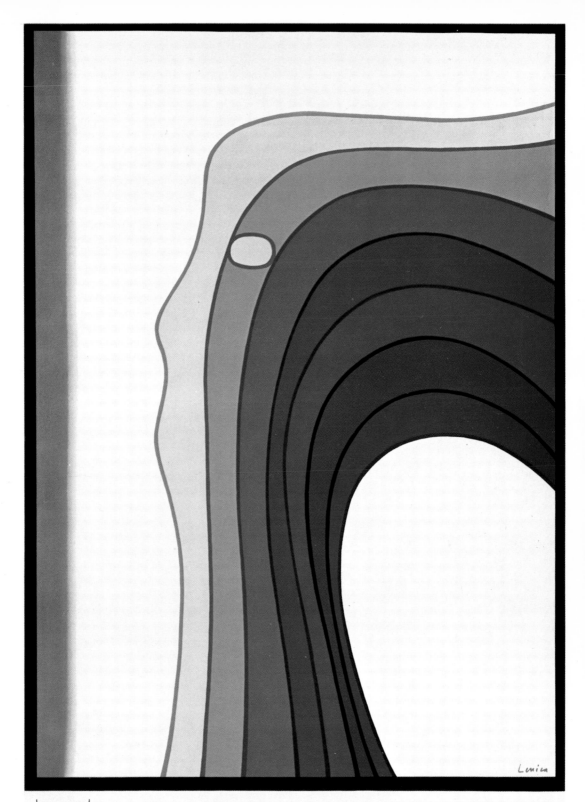

Olympische Spiele München 1972

34

35

39

36

40

37

41

38

42

43

44

45

46

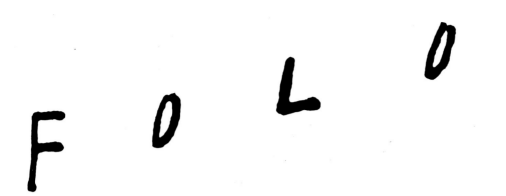

Jean-Michel Folon

Je préfère vivre à la campagne, mais je vis en ville parce que pour dire des choses sur les villes, il faut être contaminé par la ville. Sinon, on ne sait pas de quoi on parle.

Nous vivons une époque de confusion. Il y a ceux qui s'accrochent au passé et ceux qui imaginent l'avenir, et on a sous les yeux cette lutte d'un monde ancien qui disparaît et d'un monde nouveau qui nous échappe.

Tous les matins, on se lève et on sort dans la rue. Un feu rouge s'allume, il faut s'arrêter, on traverse la rue entre deux rangées de clous et des signes indiquent qu'il ne faut pas tourner à gauche, mais continuer tout droit. Toute la journée on obéit à des ordres, il y va de notre vie. Si un feu rouge s'allume et qu'on ne s'arrête pas, on est mort. Le soir on rentre chez soi épuisé, on ne sait pas pourquoi.

Un jour, avec Colette, en allant à Bruxelles, nous nous sommes mis à compter les flèches. A la moitié du trajet, du côté de Laon, nous en avions dénombré plus de six cents. Alors, j'ai compris l'importance qu'elles avaient dans notre vie. Et que la terre était un laby-

I prefer living in the country, but I live in the city because if you want to make statements about cities you have to be contaminated by them. Otherwise you do not know what you are speaking about.

We live in an age of chaos. Some people cling to the past and others dream of the future, and we see before us a struggle between an old world that is disappearing and a new world that is eluding us.

Every morning one gets up and goes out into the street. When a red lamp lights up you have to stop, and you cross the street between two rows of nails and signs stating that you must not turn left, but must go straight on. All day long you are obeying orders because your life depends on it. If a red lamp lights up and you do not stop, you are dead. At night you come home exhausted and you do not know why.

One day, on the way to Brussels with Colette, we started counting road signs. At the half-way stage, about Laon, we had got beyond 600. It was then that I began to understand the importance they have in our lives. I began to under-

Ich würde lieber auf dem Land wohnen, aber ich wohne in der Stadt, denn um über die Stadt etwas sagen zu können, muß man sich von ihr infizieren lassen. Sonst weiß man ja nicht, wovon man spricht.

Wir leben in einem Zeitalter der Verwirrung. Die einen klammern sich an die Vergangenheit, die anderen malen sich die Zukunft aus, und vor unseren Augen spielt sich dieser Kampf zwischen einer alten, sterbenden und einer neuen Welt ab, die sich uns noch entzieht.

Jeden Morgen steht man auf und betritt die Straße. Ein rotes Licht blinkt auf — man muß stehenbleiben. Man muß die Straße auf den Zebrastreifen überqueren, und Zeichen geben an, daß man sich nicht nach links wenden darf, sondern geradeaus weitergehen soll. Den ganzen Tag gehorcht man Befehlen. Leben und Tod hängen davon ab. Wenn ein rotes Licht aufleuchtet und man nicht stehenbleibt, so ist man tot. Abends kehrt man heim, erschöpft — man weiß nicht recht weshalb.

Als ich eines Tages mit Colette

Jean-Michel Folon

rinthe, et je me suis mis à les regarder de plus près. On peut les regarder en fonction d'un pays. Par exemple, en Italie, les flèches sont des suggestions, «vous pouvez aller par là», en Allemagne, ce sont des ordres et en Amérique elles sont d'une lisibilité immédiate parce que la vie y est tellement rapide qu'elles vous disent, «si vous ne suivez pas cette direction, vous êtes mort». Parce que vous perdez une heure et que là-bas, perdre une heure, c'est être mort.

Une nuit, il faudrait enlever tous les signes de la surface de la terre et voir qui arriverait le lendemain matin.

Un dessin doit rester le plus ouvert possible, parce qu'un dessin c'est un prétexte à l'imagination du lecteur.

stand that the earth is a labyrinth, and I started to take a closer look at it. You can look at road signs in relation to a particular country. For example, in Italy the signs suggest, "You could go that way"; in Germany they are orders; and in America they are legible and urgent because life goes past so fast that, as they say, "If you do not follow this instruction you will be dead". The reason is that you would waste an hour, and in America wasting an hour means being dead.

It would be a good thing one night to take away all the signs on the earth's surface and see what happens the following morning.

A design must be kept as imprecise as possible, because a design is an opportunity for the imagination of the viewer.

nach Brüssel fuhr, begannen wir die Richtungspfeile zu zählen. Auf halber Strecke, in der Nähe von Laon, waren wir schon auf mehr als 600 gekommen. Damals begriff ich, welche Bedeutung ihnen in unserem Leben zukommt, und daß die Welt ein Labyrinth ist — und ich begann, mir die Richtungspfeile näher anzusehen. Man kann sie als Ausdruck des Nationalcharakters eines Landes betrachten. In Italien z.B. sind die Pfeile Aufforderungen wie: «Sie können diese Richtung nehmen.» In Deutschland dagegen sind sie Befehle, und in Amerika sind sie von suggestiver Eindringlichkeit, weil das Leben dort so hastig ist, daß sie einem sagen: «Wenn du nicht dieser Richtung folgst, bist du tot»; weil man sonst eine Stunde verlieren könnte, und weil eine Stunde verlieren, dort tot sein heißt.

Man sollte in einer Nacht alle Zeichen von der Erdoberfläche entfernen und sehen, was am nächsten Morgen geschehen würde. Eine Zeichnung sollte möglichst offen bleiben, damit sie als Anreiz auf die Phantasie des Betrachters wirkt.

Jean-Michel Folon

1934	Né à Bruxelles.	*1934*	*Born at Brussels.*	1934	In Brüssel geboren.
1965	Reçoit le Grand Prix de la «Troisième Triennale de l'humour dans l'Art», Italie.	*1965*	*Awarded the Grand Prix of the third Triennale of humor in art, Italy.*	1965	Erhält den «Großen Preis der Dritten Triennale des Humors in der Kunst».
1966	Reçoit le «Certificate of Merit» décerné par le «Art Directors Club», New York.	*1966*	*Awarded the Certificate of Merit by the Art Directors Club, New York.*	1966	Wird mit dem «Certificate of Merit» vom New Yorker «Art Directors Club» ausgezeichnet.
1967	Expose à la «Cinquième Biennale de Paris». Travaille au film de William Klein «Qui êtes-vous, Polly Maggoo ?». Réalise un film avec Alain Resnais «Le Cri». Travaille régulièrement avec Olivetti, Italie. En collaboration avec Giorgio Soavi, réalise le livre «Le Message».	*1967*	*Exhibited at the fifth Paris Biennale. Worked on the William Klein film "Who Are You, Polly Maggoo?". Made the film "Le Cri" with Alain Resnais. Worked regularly for Olivetti, Italy. Designed the book "Le Message" in collaboration with Giorgio Soavi.*	1967	Stellt auf der «Cinquième Biennale de Paris» aus. Mitarbeiter an William Kleins Film «Qui êtes-vous, Polly Maggoo ?». Realisiert den Film «Le Cri» mit Alain Resnais. Arbeitet regelmäßig für Olivetti. Gestaltet das Buch «Le Message» in Zusammenarbeit mit Giorgio Soavi.
1968	Tourne un film d'animation pour le Service de la recherche de la Télévision Française. Peint sur verre un billard lumineux pour le film de William Klein «Mister Freedom». Dessine un livre édité par le «Museum of Modern Art» de New York. Réalise pour la «Triennale de Milan» une surface lumineuse animée de 36 m².	*1968*	*Made an animated film for the French Television research department. Painted a luminous pin-table on glass for the William Klein film "Mister Freedom". Designed a book published by the Museum of Modern Art, New York. Designed an animated luminous surface with an area of 36 sq. meters for the Milan Triennale.*	1968	Dreht einen Zeichenfilm für den Suchdienst des französischen Fernsehens. Malt für William Kleins Film «Mister Freedom» einen leuchtenden Billardtisch auf Glas. Illustriert ein vom Museum of Modern Art in New York herausgegebenes Buch. Zeichnet für die Mailänder Triennale eine Leuchtfarbfläche von 36 m²
1969	Expose à la «Lefebre Gallery», New York.	*1969*	*Exhibited at the Lefebre Gallery, New York.*	1969	Stellt in der Lefebre Gallery, New York, aus.
1970	Travaille à un important environnement pour l'Exposition universelle d'Osaka.	*1970*	*Worked on a big layout for Expo 70, Osaka.*	1970	Arbeitet an einer umfangreichen Gestaltung für die Expo 70 in Osaka.

Jean-Michel Folon

1

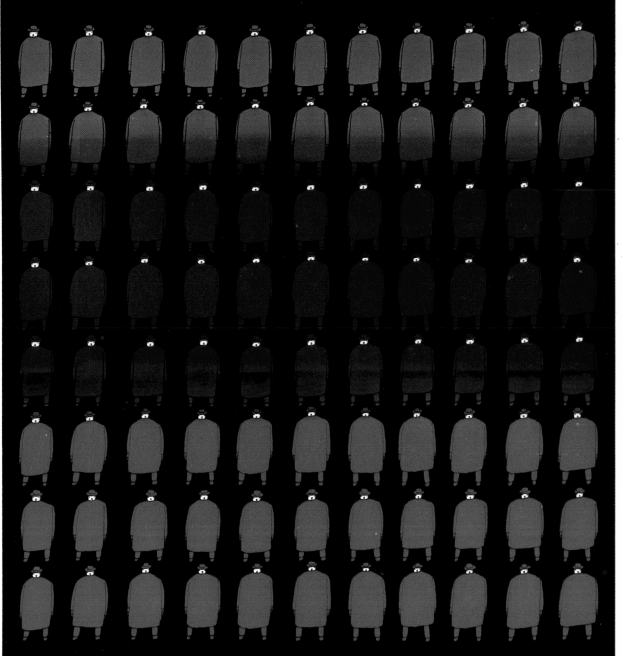

FOULTITUDE

MUSEE DES ARTS DECORATIFS

107 RUE DE RIVOLI   PARIS 1   DU 26 MARS AU 5 MAI 1969

prisme
international
3

Revue d'Arts graphiques
et communications visuelles

A rich review of graphic art
and visuels communications

Französische Zeit
und visuelle Kommunikation

FOLON

Design

245 May 1969 5s

Awards for posters/Graphics by Jean-Michel Folon/Wates selling centre

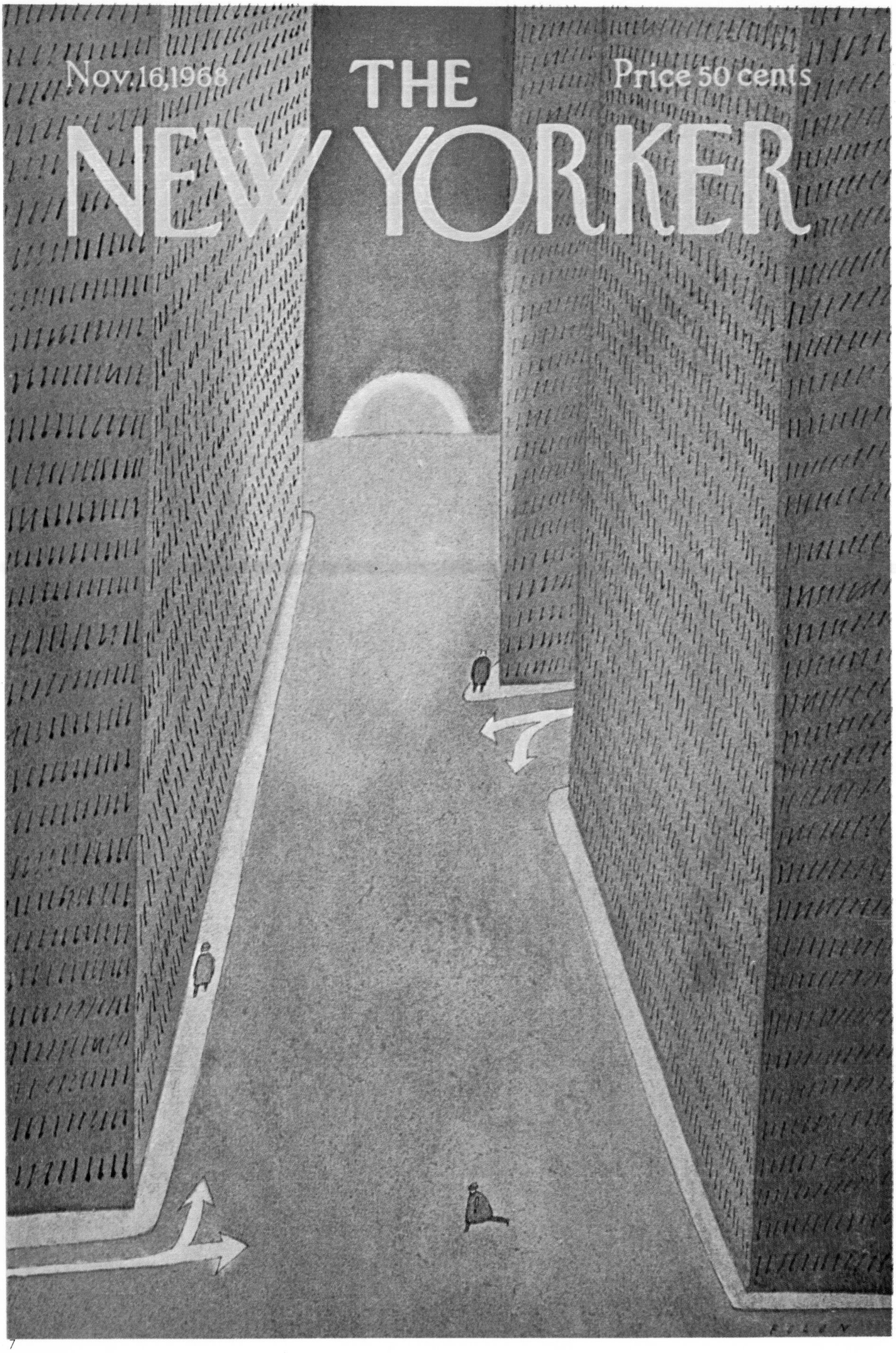
Nov. 16, 1968
THE
NEW YORKER
Price 50 cents

THE NEW YORKER

Price 50 cents

olivetti   ОЛИВЕТТИ   أوليفتي   ९१⼗ʌ⼁ム६   आलिवेत्ति   オリベッティ   Ὀλιβέττι

At least talk to each other.
To communicate is the beginning of understanding. AT&T

10

Reach out for someone.
To communicate is the beginning of understanding. AT&T

11

13

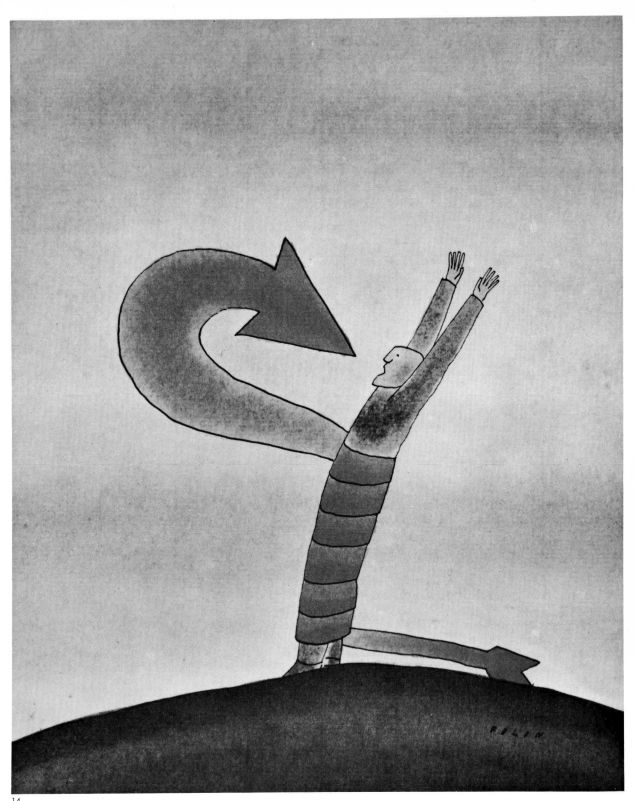

14

15

16

17

18

19

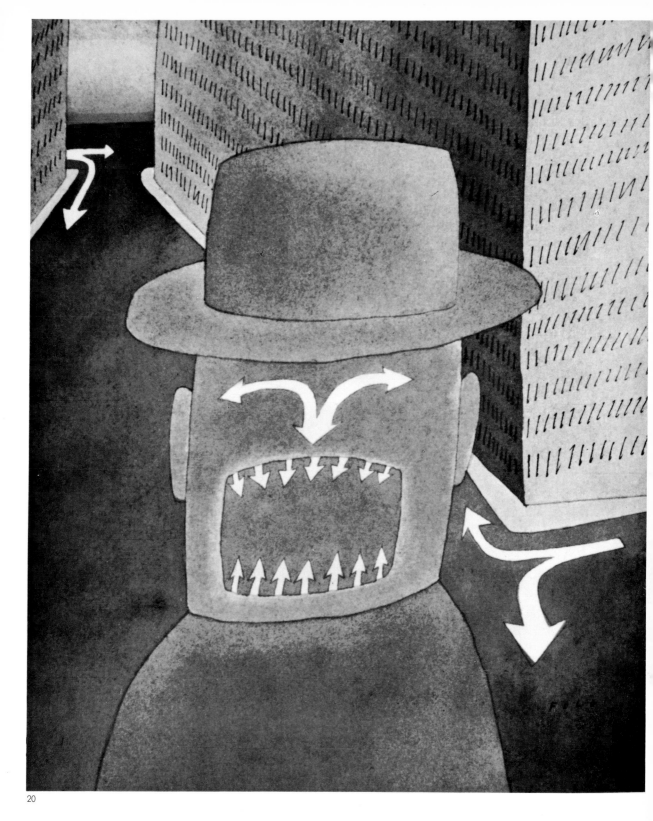

20

Josef Müller-Brockmann

Il était difficile pour nos professeurs, comme il l'est pour nous, d'imaginer le monde de demain en fonction de l'évolution scientifique. De plus, des préjugés nationaux, politiques, raciaux, religieux, ne facilitent pas le dialogue sur le plan international.

Si l'on constate que le tiers de la population mondiale meurt de faim et que, un milliard et demi de gens vivent de façon inhumaine, nous nous rendons compte que la survie de notre planète dépend de l'attitude des gouvernements face à ces problèmes. Nous n'en sommes pas personnellement conscients, dans notre travail quotidien, quoique par notre pensée et notre activité nous pourrions contribuer, aussi modestement soit-il, à une amélioration. Il serait donc souhaitable que nous conjuguions nos efforts pour éduquer la nouvelle génération, de telle sorte qu'elle ait des dispositions d'esprit qui l'encourage à faire passer le bien-être général avant ses propres intérêts. Tous les efforts de culture et d'éducation devraient, par conséquent, tendre à trouver une harmonie entre le plan national et international.

It was as difficult for our teachers as it is for us to imagine tomorrow's world in its relation to scientific developments. Additionally, national, political, racial and religious prejudices do not facilitate dialogues at an international level.

If it is assumed to be true that one-third of the world's population is starving and that one and a half milliard people are living in conditions unworthy of human beings, it would appear to follow that the survival of this planet depends upon the attitude of governments to these problems. We are not aware of these things in our daily work but we are capable of helping, however modestly, by thought and action. It would therefore seem desirable to try to indoctrinate the younger generation to induce in them an attitude of mind that puts the general welfare before their own interests. The logical consequence of this would be aimed at achieving harmony between national and international levels.

Up to the present time, creative design would not seem to have endowed functional shape with significance. During his training,

Es war schwierig für unsere Lehrer wie auch für uns, sich die Welt von morgen in Abhängigkeit des wissenschaftlichen Fortschritts vorzustellen. Dazu kommt, daß staatliche, politische, rassistische und religiöse Vorurteile den Dialog auf internationaler Ebene noch erschweren.

Wenn man bedenkt, daß ein Drittel der Weltbevölkerung Hunger leidet und Hungers stirbt, und daß ein-einhalb Milliarden Menschen ein Leben in Armut und Elend führen, wird man sich darüber klar, daß das Überleben auf unserem Planeten von der Haltung der Regierungen zu diesem Problem abhängt. Persönlich sind wir uns dessen in unserem Alltagsleben nicht bewußt, obwohl wir durch unsere Denkweise und unsere Handlungen das Unsrige zu einer, wenn auch noch so bescheidenen Besserung beitragen könnten. Es wäre deshalb wünschenswert, daß wir unsere Anstrengungen vereinen würden, um die neue Generation so zu erziehen, daß ihre Geisteshaltung sie, wenn es um das Wohl der Allgemeinheit geht, zur Zurückstellung des eigenen Ichs veranlassen wür-

61

Josef Müller-Brockmann

La création graphique ne semble pas, jusqu'à ce jour, avoir donné à l'image fonctionnelle une signification. Au cours de ses études, le graphiste apprend à établir le lien entre le producteur et le consommateur au moyen d'une image conventionnelle.

Sa conception de la communication l'amène à trouver des solutions pour vendre «au mieux» des idées ou des produits. L'enseignement actuel porte l'accent sur l'idée originale et l'impact de la composition. Il néglige l'étude de la société dans laquelle nous vivons et notamment sa demande légitime d'objectivité dans l'information publicitaire. Il s'attache plus à la forme graphique qu'à sa signification profonde. Lorsque l'étude de cette expression sera assumée par l'éducation, la forme de la composition se modifiera de façon très nette. S'il s'agit simplement d'annoncer un bon produit ou une idée positive, il sera suffisant de placer l'un ou l'autre au centre de la composition.

L'information atteindra un maximum d'expression si l'objet ou l'idée sont présentés de façon esthétique et efficiente, avec un minimum de formes d'accompagnement. Aussi bien l'ornement

subjectif, dans le sens d'une exagération illustrative, qu'une présentation par trop objective sont à éviter. La forme graphique doit, si possible, devenir véhicule anonyme du message à transmettre. Cette conception donne à l'artiste une nouvelle optique.

Avec les ressources de la science

the draftsman learns to establish a link between producers and consumers by means of a conventional image.

His concept of communication leads him to aim at those designs that "best" sell the ideas or products concerned. Present teaching places its emphasis on original ideas and the impact of the composition. It neglects the study of the society in which we live and in particular its legitimate right to objectivity in publicity information. It pays more attention to graphic form than to its deeper significance. When the educators take up the study of this aspect, the form of composition will be clearly modified. If all that is necessary to publicize a good product or a positive idea, it will suffice to make the item concerned the center of the composition. The message will reach a maximum power of expression if the object or idea is presented aesthetically and efficiently with a minimum of accompanying design. Both subjective ornament in the sense of illustrative exaggerations and over-objective presentation must be avoided. Graphics should if possible become an anonymous vehicle for the message to be transmitted. This concept gives the artist a new angle of vision.

A draftsman can use the resources of science and technology to provide a clear view of the interior structure of things and the basis of their specific meanings.

The optical, acoustic, kinetic, and spatial aspects of these possibilities in composition are novel and fascinating. The verbal text is given a convincing and interesting pictorial support.

In every field of artistic research, creative individuals are in a position to express their concepts, by all the means available to them, with both present and future validity.

Once the problem of informing has been solved on the practical, objective, and aesthetic levels, the

de. Alle kulturellen und erzieherischen Bemühungen sollten folglich darauf abzielen, eine Harmonie auf der nationalen und der internationalen Ebene zu finden.

Die Graphik scheint bis zum heutigen Tag der funktionellen Darstellung keine Bedeutung beigemessen zu haben. Im Laufe seiner Studien lernt der Graphiker, mittels einer konventionellen Darstellung, eine Verbindung zwischen dem Produzenten und dem Konsumenten herzustellen.

Seine Vorstellungen über die Kommunikation veranlassen ihn, Möglichkeiten zu finden, um Ideen und Produkte «bestmöglich» zu verkaufen. Der heutige Unterricht legt das Schwergewicht auf die originelle Idee und die Schlagkraft der Komposition. Er vernachlässigt das Studium der Gesellschaft, in der er und wir leben und insbesondere deren gerechtfertigte Forderung nach Objektivität in der Information.

Er ist an die graphische Form statt an deren tiefere Bedeutung gebunden. Erst wenn das Studium dieses Ausdrucks Teil der Erziehung geworden sein wird, wird die Form der Komposition sich ändern. Wenn es sich einfach darum handelt, ein gutes Produkt oder eine positive Idee anzukündigen, wird es genügen, das eine oder andere in den Mittelpunkt der Komposition zu setzen.

Die Information wird ein Maximum an Ausdruck erhalten, wenn das Objekt oder die Idee auf ästhetische und wirkungsvolle Weise und mit einem Minimum an Begleitformen dargeboten werden wird. Eine subjektive Verzierung im Sinne einer illustrativen Übertreibung, sowie eine allzu objektive Darstellung müssen vermieden werden. Die graphische Form muß, wenn möglich, zum anonymen Träger der zu übermittelnden Botschaft werden. Diese Haltung öffnet dem Künstler neue Perspektiven.

Der Graphiker kann mit den Mitteln der Wissenschaft und der Technik

Josef Müller-Brockmann

et de la technologie, le graphiste peut démontrer avec clarté la structure intérieure des choses et la base de leur signification spécifique.

Les aspects optiques, acoustiques, cynétiques et spaciaux de ces possibilités dans la composition sont nouveaux et fascinants. Le commentaire écrit reçoit un support pictural qui à la fois convainc et intéresse.

Dans tous les domaines de la recherche artistique, les créateurs sont à même d'exprimer, par tous les moyens, ce qu'ils ont conçu, aussi bien pour le présent que pour le futur.

Lorsque le problème d'information est résolu sur un plan pratique, objectif et esthétique, le langage de la forme fera éclater sa compréhension traditionnelle, pour devenir un langage universel.

C'est dans ce sens que certains signes laissent envisager le futur; souhaitons qu'ils deviennent rapidement réalité!

language of form will burst the bounds of traditional understanding and become a universal language.
It is in this direction that the pointers to the future lead. Let us hope that they will rapidly produce reality.

die innere Struktur der Dinge und die Basis ihrer spezifischen Bedeutung deutlich machen.

Die optischen, akustischen, kinetischen und räumlichen Darstellungsmöglichkeiten der Komposition sind neu und faszinierend. Der geschriebene Kommentar erhält einen optischen Akzent, welcher gleichzeitig überzeugt und interessiert. Auf allen Gebieten des künstlerischen Schaffens sind die Künstler imstande, mit allen Mitteln auszudrücken, was sie für die Gegenwart wie auch für die Zukunft erkannt haben. Wenn das Problem der Information auf einer praktischen, objektiven und ästhetischen Ebene gelöst sein wird, wird die Sprache der Form ihre traditionelle Fassungskraft zum bersten bringen, um zu einer universellen Sprache zu werden. In diesem Sinne lassen gewisse Symptome die Zukunft erahnen: Hoffentlich werden sie bald Wirklichkeit.

Josef Müller-Brockmann

1914	Né à Rapperswil, canton de Saint-Gall, Suisse. Fait deux ans d'apprentissage chez A.W. Diggelman, à Zurich. Suit, comme auditeur, durant deux ans les cours de l'Ecole des Arts décoratifs de Zurich. Suit les cours de l'Université et de l'Ecole Polytechnique fédérale de Zurich.	*1914*

1914 — Né à Rapperswil, canton de Saint-Gall, Suisse. Fait deux ans d'apprentissage chez A.W. Diggelman, à Zurich. Suit, comme auditeur, durant deux ans les cours de l'Ecole des Arts décoratifs de Zurich. Suit les cours de l'Université et de l'Ecole Polytechnique fédérale de Zurich.

1936 — S'installe comme graphiste indépendant.

1939 — Dessine le secteur des universités de Suisse, à l'Exposition nationale de Zurich.

1939-1957 — Création du pavillon suisse à Paris, Copenhague, New York, Barcelone, Prague, Utrecht, etc. Création de nombreuses expositions dans plusieurs villes de Suisse. Créations pour la scène à Munich, Zurich et Copenhague.

1952 — Création de marionnettes pour «Hin und Zurück» de Hindemith à Zurich.

1956-1959 — Vice-président puis président du «Verband Schweizerischer Graphiker».

1957-1960 — Est appelé comme maître de graphisme à l'Ecole des Arts décoratifs de Zurich.

1958 — Edite et rédige le périodique «Neue Grafik».

1964 — Participe à la création du secteur «Science et recherche», à l'Exposition nationale suisse (architecte Max Bill).

1965 — Fonde la «Galerie 58 für konkrete Kunst» à Rapperswil.

1914 — Born at Rapperswil, Canton St. Gall, Switzerland.
Trained for two years with A.W. Diggelmann at Zurich. Studied for two years at the Zurich Kunstgewerbeschule. Attended courses at Zurich University and the Federal Institute of Technology.

1936 — Set up as an independent designer.

1939 — Designed the Swiss Universities section at the Zurich National Exhibition.

1939-57 — Designed Swiss Pavilions at Paris, Copenhagen, New York, Barcelona, Prague, Utrecht, and elsewhere. Designed numerous exhibitions in various Swiss cities. Designed stage scenery in Munich, Zurich, and Copenhagen.

1952 — Designed the marionettes for Hindemith's "Hin und Zurück", Zurich.

1956-59 — Vice-president and then president of the Verband Schweizerischer Graphiker.

1957-60 — Draftsmanship instructor at the Zurich Kunstgewerbeschule.

1958 — Published and edited the periodical "Neue Grafik".

1964 — Took part in designing the section on science and research at the Swiss National Exhibition (architect Max Bill).

1965 — Established the Galerie 58 für konkrete Kunst, Rapperswil.

1914 — In Rapperswil (St. Gallen), Schweiz, geboren. Zweijährige Lehre bei A.W. Diggelmann, Zürich, und Besuch der Kurse an der «Kunstgewerbeschule», Zürich. Hört Vorlesungen an der Universität Zürich und an der Eidgenössischen Technischen Hochschule.

1936 — Beginn seiner selbständigen künstlerischen Tätigkeit.

1939 — Entwirft den Sektor der Schweizerischen Universitäten an der Landesausstellung in Zürich.

1939-57 — Gestaltung der Schweizer Pavillons in Paris, Kopenhagen, New York, Barcelona, Prag, Utrecht, usw. sowie vieler Ausstellungen in mehreren Schweizer Städten. Bühnenbildner in München, Zürich und Kopenhagen. Entwurf und Anfertigung von Marionetten für «Hin und Zurück» von Hindemith.

1956-59 — Zunächst Vizepräsident, dann Präsident des Verbandes schweizerischer Graphiker.

1957-60 — Wird als Lehrer an die Graphik-Klasse der Kunstgewerbeschule Zürich berufen.

1958 — Redaktor und Herausgeber der Zeitschrift «Neue Graphik».

1964 — Wirkt an der Gestaltung des Sektors «Wissenschaft und Forschung» der EXPO 64 in Lausanne mit (Architekt: Max Bill).

1965 — Gründet die «Galerie 58 für konkrete Kunst» in Rapperswil.

Membre d'associations suisses et internationales dans le domaine de l'art graphique, de la typographie et de l'esthétique industrielle.
Participe à de nombreux congrès internationaux, à Tokyo, Carbon-

Member of Swiss and international associations of graphic art, typography, and industrial design.
Has taken part in numerous international congresses at Bled, Carbondale, San Marino, Tokyo, and

Mitglied schweizerischer und internationaler Vereinigungen auf dem Gebiet der graphischen Kunst, der Typographie und der Industrie-Formgebung.
Teilnahme an vielen internationa-

Josef Müller-Brockmann

dale, Bled, San Marino, etc. Se rend comme conférencier, à Tokyo, Osaka et Ulm.
Membre du jury pour «Die gute Industrieform» à Hanovre et la «Biennale de l'Affiche» à Varsovie. Expose ses travaux en Suisse, en Allemagne, au Japon et aux Etats-Unis.

elsewhere. Has read papers at Osaka, Tokyo, and Ulm.
Member of the jury of Die gute Industrieform at Hanover and at the Warsaw biennial poster exhibition. Has exhibited work in Germany, Japan, Switzerland, and the United States.

len Kongressen (in Tokio, Carbondale, Bled, San Marino, usw.). Vorträge in Tokio, Osaka, Ulm. Mitglied der Jury für «Die gute Industrieform» in Hannover und für die «Biennale des Plakats» in Warschau. Ausstellung seiner Arbeiten in der Schweiz, in Deutschland, Japan und USA.

Josef Müller-Brockmann

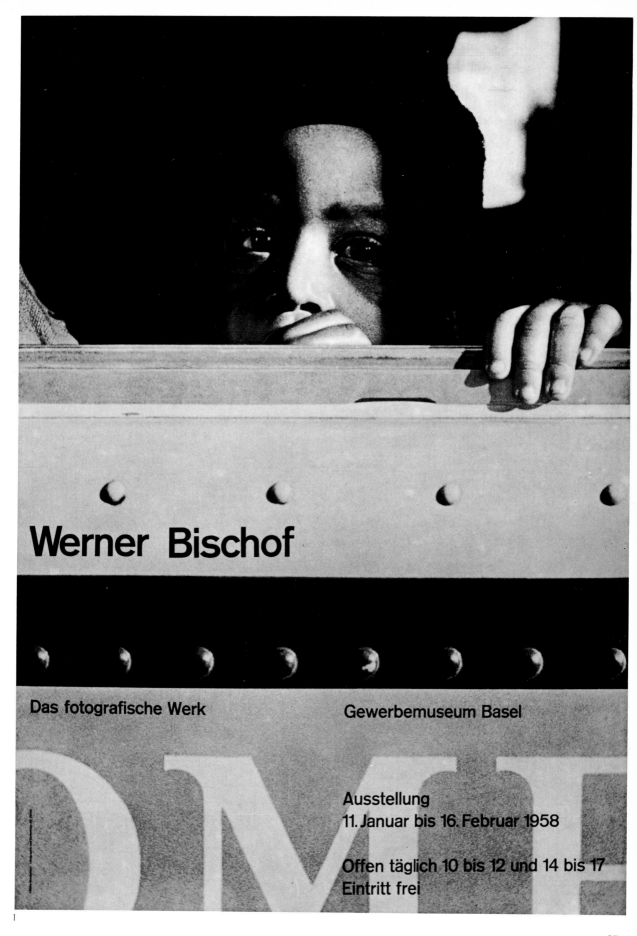

Werner Bischof

Das fotografische Werk

Gewerbemuseum Basel

Ausstellung
11. Januar bis 16. Februar 1958

Offen täglich 10 bis 12 und 14 bis 17
Eintritt frei

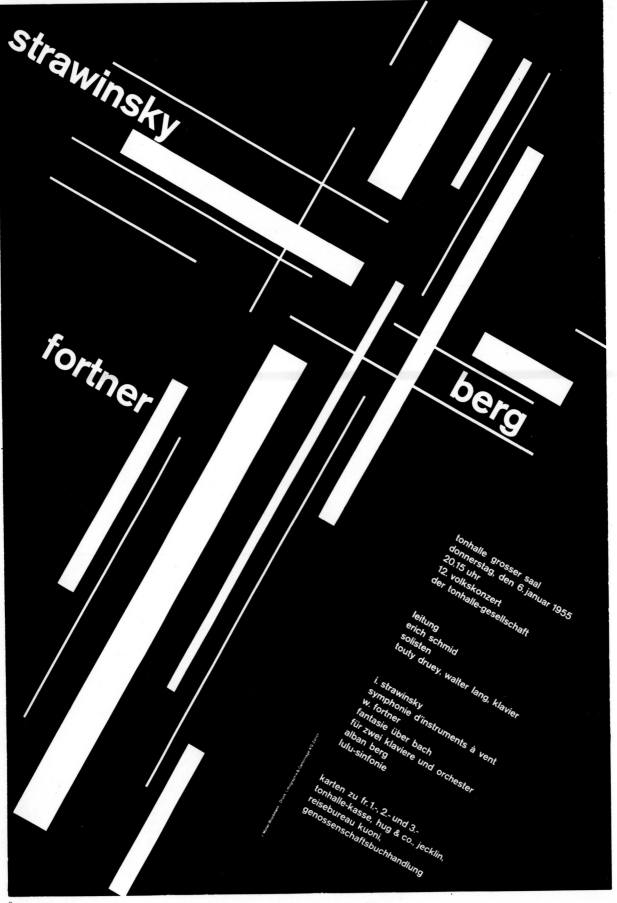

strawinsky

berg

fortner

tonhalle, grosser saal
donnerstag, den 6. januar 1955
20.15 uhr
12. volkskonzert
der tonhalle-gesellschaft

leitung
erich schmid
solisten
touty druey, walter lang, klavier

i. strawinsky
symphonie d'instruments à vent
w. fortner
fantasie über bach
für zwei klaviere und orchester
alban berg
lulu-sinfonie

karten zu fr. 1.-, 2.- und 3.-
tonhalle-kasse, hug & co., jecklin,
reisebureau kuoni,
genossenschaftsbuchhandlung

j. müller-brockmann   druck: lithographie & cartonnage AG zürich

juni-festwochen zürich
1959

tonhalle grosser saal
donnerstag
25. juni 1959, 20.15 uhr

4. konzert der tonhalle-
gesellschaft zürich
leitung
andré cluytens
solist
ricardo odnoposoff

joseph haydn
sinfonie in d-dur, mirakel-
johannes brahms
violinkonzert in d-dur
modest mussorgsky
bilder einer ausstellung

instrumentiert von
maurice ravel

karten fr. 5.50 bis 16.50
vorverkauf: tonhalle
hug, jecklin, kuoni

3

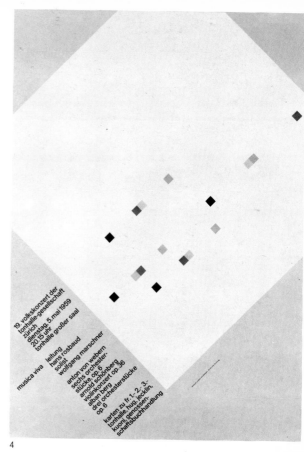

19. volkskonzert der
tonhalle-gesellschaft
zürich
dienstag 5. mai 1959
20.15 uhr
tonhalle großer saal

musica viva

leitung
hans rosbaud
solist
wolfgang marschner

anton von webern
sechs orchester-
stücke op. 6
arnold schönberg
violinkonzert op. 36
alban berg
drei orchesterstücke
op. 6

karten zu fr. 1.- 2.- 3.-
tonhalle hug, jecklin,
kuoni genossen-
schaftsbuchhandlung

4

musica viva

tonhalle kleiner saal
donnerstag
28. februar 20.15 uhr
1957

tonhalle-
gesellschaft zürich

paul hindemith
sonate für viola
und klavier
pierre boulez
«le marteau sans
maître»
text von rené clair
béla bartók
sonate
für zwei klaviere
und schlagzeug

solisten
sibylle plate gesang
maria bergmann
und hans rosbaud
klavier
albert dietrich viola
kraft-thorwald dilloo
flöte
anton stingl gitarre

karlheinz bender
robert hänggeli
adolf neumeier
fritz zimmermann
schlagzeug
erich seiler schlag-
zeug und vibraphon

vorverkauf tonhalle
hug jecklin kuoni
karten fr. 3.30–7.70

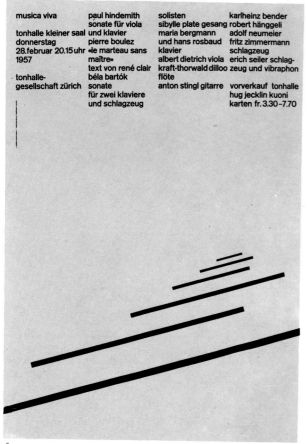

5

beethoven

tonhalle   grosser saal
            dienstag, den 22. februar 1955,
            20.15 uhr
            4. extrakonzert
            der tonhalle-gesellschaft
leitung   carl schuricht
solist   wolfgang schneiderhan
beethoven   ouverture zu «coriolan», op. 62
            violinkonzert in d-dur, op. 61
            siebente sinfonie in a-dur, op. 92
vorverkauf tonhalle-kasse, hug, jecklin,
            kuoni
            karten zu fr. 3.50 bis 9.50

6

végh-quartett musica viva

paul hindemith
alban berg
béla bartók

1. kammermusikabend der tonhalle-gesellschaft
zürich, donnerstag, den 30. okt. 1958, 20.15 uhr
kleiner tonhalle-saal

paul hindemith drittes streichquartett
alban berg   lyrische suite
béla bartók   viertes streichquartett

karten zu fr. 3.30–7.70
vorverkauf tonhalle-kasse, hug, jecklin, kuoni
dep. kasse oerlikon der schweiz. kreditanstalt

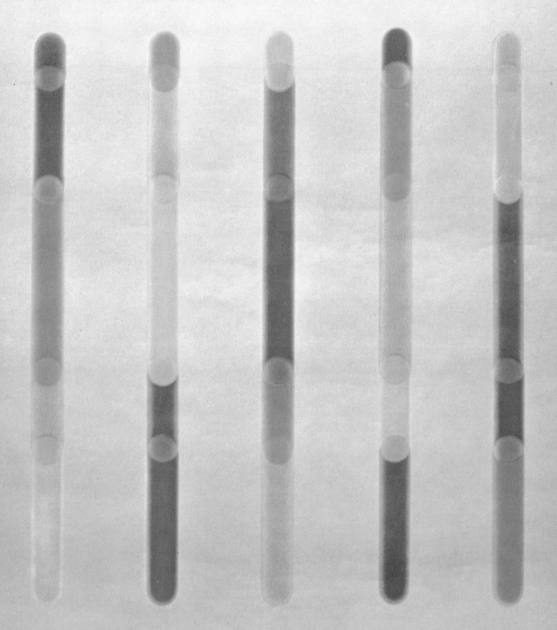

georg solti, claudio arrau
brahms, beethoven, schumann

**erstes juni-festkonzert 1960 der tonhalle-gesellschaft zürich, donnerstag, 2. juni
20.15 uhr, grosser tonhallesaal. leitung: georg solti, solist: claudio arrau.
brahms: haydn-variationen, beethoven: fünftes klavierkonzert in es-dur,
schumann: vierte sinfonie in d-moll. karten zu fr. 5.50 bis 16.50, tonhallekasse,
hug, kuoni, jecklin, depositenkasse oerlikon kreditanstalt**

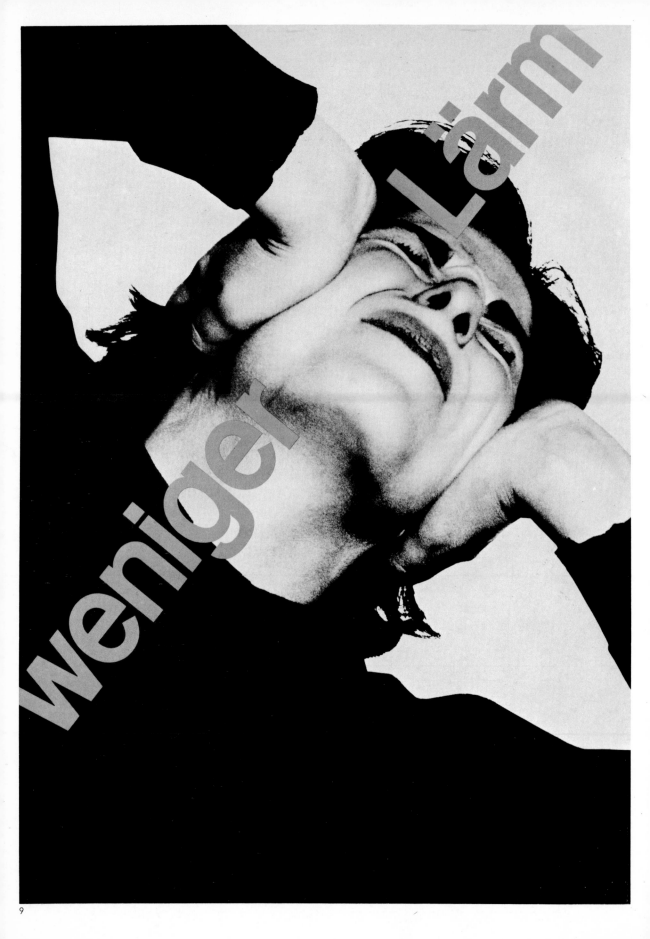

weniger Lärm

10

11

12

13

Kunstgewerbemuseum Zürich
Ausstellung

der Film

10. Januar bis 30. April 1960

Offen: Montag 14-18, 20-22
Dienstag-Freitag 10-12, 14-18, 20-22
Samstag-Sonntag 10-12, 14-17

tonhalle-
gesellschaft zürich
juni-festwochen

dienstag	2. juni 1964	karl böhm, dietrich fischer-dieskau; werke von beethoven, mahler, strauss
dienstag	9. juni 1964	wolfgang sawallisch, zino francescatti; werke von brahms, dvorak
dienstag	16. juni 1964	joseph keilberth, robert casadesus; werke von mozart, bruckner
dienstag	23. juni 1964	john barbirolli, van cliburn; werke von wagner, tschaikowsky, sibelius
dienstag	30. juni 1964	jean martinon, henryk szeryng; werke von beethoven, martinon, brahms
		extra-volkskonzert:
sonntag	7. juni 1964	hans erismann, maria stader, verena gohl, ernst häfliger, peter lagger, sängerverein harmonie; schibler: media in vita

sinfonie-
konzerte

15

16

Wohlstand für alle

17

18

19

20

21

22

23

24

25

warum   wie   wer   wo

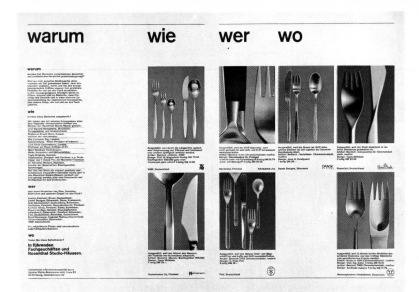

26

warum   wie   wer   wo

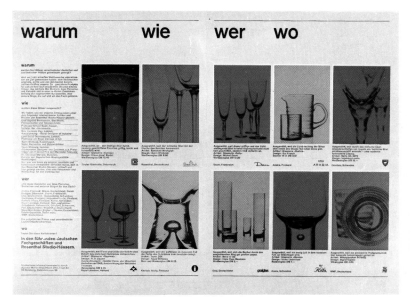

27

warum   wie   wer   wo

28

29

30

31

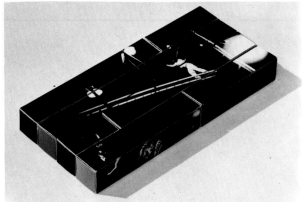

32

Une bonne marque peut être un signe de reconnaissance très efficace pour une entreprise, institution, exposition ou spectacle, rendant superflue tout autre explication. Quelques données indispensables doivent être observées.

La marque-image doit être lapidaire, simple, le symbole contraignant du thème ou de l'objet, d'une forme facile à comprendre, facile à retenir. Elle doit être unique, sans ressemblance avec les marques existantes. Elle doit figurer sur tous les supports de la publicité: en-têtes de lettres, plaques d'adresses, voitures de livraison, annonces, imprimés, publicité lumineuse. Elle doit s'harmoniser avec toute action publicitaire. Dans ces conditions, la marque a un effet constant qui ne risque pas de s'affaiblir.

La marque-lettre doit reproduire le nom d'une entreprise, institution, exposition etc. dans une forme caractéristique. Alors le risque sera moindre d'être mal compris puisque la marque-lettre s'explique d'elle-même. La suite et la forme des lettres la rendent facilement saisissable. Ces avantages diminuent avec les plus forts agrandissements ou réductions qui entravent la lisibilité.

Le visage de l'entreprise

Ces marques ne rentrent pas toujours aisément dans la construction d'une conception publicitaire. Il est donc recommandé de composer le nom d'une maison d'éléments purement typographiques et de conserver cette solution dans tous les moyens publicitaires. De cette manière la forme typographique peut façonner le caractère général d'une maison et en devenir l'expression la plus marquante. Tous les imprimés peuvent alors être composés dans la même famille de caractères. Cette unité de moyens permet les applications les plus larges, la conception publicitaire est plus aisée, l'absence de clichés abaisse le prix de revient.

La conception publicitaire, bâtie avec les seuls éléments typographiques, assure par ses effets de répétition, de cumulation, l'unité de la forme et de l'effet; elle sera ainsi à la fois variée et persuasive.

fincolor finalba

33

Jedes Jahr wird eine Vielzahl von Ausstellungen veranstaltet und meistens wird der Grafiker mit der optischen Gestaltung beauftragt. Von seiner Fähigkeit, ein Thema übersichtlich zu ordnen und darzustellen, hängt zu einem grossen Teil der Werbeerfolg ab.

34

35

1. orchesterkonzert

mittwoch, den 4. juni 1969
leitung/ erich leinsdorf
solist/ isaac stern, violine
c. m. v. weber/ freischütz-ouvertüre
l. van beethoven/ violinkonzert in d-dur, op. 61
igor strawinsky/ le sacre du printemps

extrakonzert

sonntag, den 8. juni 1969
isaac stern, violine
alexander zakin, klavier
werke von   bach
brahms
prokofieff
bartok

2. orchesterkonzert

dienstag, den 10. juni 1969
leitung/ antal dorati
solist/ claudio arrau, klavier
joseph haydn/ sinfonie in b-dur, nr. 98
richard strauss/ till eulenspiegels lustige streiche, op. 28
johannes brahms/ klavierkonzert in d-moll, op. 15

musica viva-konzert

dienstag, den 12. juni 1969
duo alfons und aloys kontarsky, klavier
christoph caskel, schlagzeug
werke von bernd a. zimmermann
earl brown
karlheinz stockhausen
pierre boulez

konzerte
junifestwochen   1969

tonhalle—
gesellschaft
zürich

3. orchesterkonzert

dienstag, den 17. juni 1969
leitung/ rudolf kempe
solist/ zino francescatti, violine
karl amadeus hartmann/
kammerkonzert für klarinette, streichquartett
und streichorchester (uraufführung)
felix mendelssohn/ violinkonzert in e-moll, op. 64
l. van beethoven/ siebente sinfonie in a-dur, op. 92

2. extrakonzert

donnerstag, den 19. juni 1969
arturo benedetti michelangeli
werke von clementi
schumann
ravel

4. orchesterkonzert

dienstag, den 24. juni 1969
leitung/ wolfgang sawallisch
solist/ arthur rubinstein, klavier
arthur honegger/ monopartita
peter tschaikowsky/ klavierkonzert in b-moll, op. 23
robert schumann/ zweite sinfonie in c-dur, op. 61

5. orchesterkonzert

dienstag, den 1. juli 1969
leitung/ rudolf kempe
solisten/ christa ludwig, alt
waldemar kmentt, tenor
w. a. mozart/ sinfonie in b-dur, kv 319
gustav mahler/ das lied von der erde

vorverkauf

tonhallekasse
musikhaus hug
pianohaus jecklin
reisebureau kuoni
filiale oerlikon kreditanstalt

preise

fr. 10.- bis 35.- orchesterkonzerte
fr. 10.- bis 30.- extrakonzerte
fr. 5.- bis 11.- musica viva-konzert

v
mu s i ca
v
a

musica viva-konzert

donnerstag, 8. januar 1970
20.15 uhr
grosser tonhallesaal

12. sinfoniekonzert
der
tonhalle-gesellschaft zürich

leitung klaus huber
charles dutoit

solist györgy ligeti
karl engel igor strawinsky
klavier

tonhalle- klaus huber
orchester

«tenebrae»
für grosses orchester
1966-67
«atmosphères»
konzert
für klavier, blasinstrumente,
kontrabässe und pauke
«tenebrae»
wiederholung

karten zu fr. 1.- bis fr. 5.-

tonhallekasse, hug, jecklin, kuoni
filiale oerlikon schweiz. kreditanstalt

entwurf j. müller-brockmann / druck bollmann zürich

38

konzerte   der tonhalle-gesellschaft
                 zürich

1. konzert   donnerstag, 2. juni

leitung   sir john barbirolli
solist   zino francescatti
elgar   introduction und allegro
tschaikowskij   violinkonzert in d-dur
beethoven   fünfte sinfonie in c-moll

2. konzert   dienstag, 7. juni

leitung   joseph keilberth
solisten   herta töpper, alt
                  fritz wunderlich, tenor
schubert   sechste sinfonie in c-dur
mahler   das lied von der erde

3. konzert   dienstag, 14. juni

leitung   rudolf kempe
solist   van cliburn
willy burkhard   hymnus für orchester
prokofieff   drittes klavierkonzert in c-dur
brahms   erste sinfonie in c-moll

4. konzert   dienstag, 21. juni

leitung   jean martinon
solisten   robert, gaby und jean casadesus
haydn   sinfonie in es-dur
                  «mit dem paukenwirbel»
bach   konzert für drei klaviere in d-moll
casadesus   konzert für drei klaviere
debussy   la mer

juni-festwochen 66
tonhalle gesellschaft
zürich

5. konzert   dienstag, 28. juni

leitung   rudolf kempe
solist   henryk szeryng
weber   ouvertüre zur oper «oberon»
mendelssohn   violinkonzert in e-moll
strauss   eine alpensinfonie

kammerabend   freitag, 24. juni
kleiner tonhallesaal
leitung   hans willi haeusslein
solist   werner ernst, bass
schoeck   «elegie»

39

Juni-Festwochen

1. Orchesterkonzert
Dienstag, den 6. Juni 1967
Leitung: Otto Klemperer
Solisten:
Heather Harper, Sopran
Janet Baker, Alt
Chor:
Gemischter Chor Zürich
Gustav Mahler:
Zweite Sinfonie in c-moll

Liederabend
Donnerstag, den 8. Juni 1967
Dietrich Fischer-Dieskau
Jörg Demus (Klavier)
Schubert:
«Die schöne Müllerin»

2. Orchesterkonzert
Dienstag, den 13. Juni 1967
Leitung: Rudolf Kempe
Solist:
Arthur Rubinstein, Klavier
Ludwig van Beethoven:
Viertes Klavierkonzert in
G-dur, op. 58
Johannes Brahms:
Zweites Klavierkonzert in
B-dur, op. 83

Zürich 1967

Zeitgenössische Kammer-
musik
Donnerstag, den 15. Juni 1967
Heinz Holliger,
Oboe/Englischhorn
Ursula Holliger, Harfe
Edith Picht-Axenfeld,
Cembalo
Serge Collot, Bratsche
Jürg Wyttenbach, Klavier
Werke von Ernst Krenek,
Jürg Wyttenbach,
Heinz Holliger, Klaus Huber,
Hans-Ulrich Lehmann und
Karlheinz Stockhausen

3. Orchesterkonzert
Dienstag, den 20. Juni 1967
Leitung: William Steinberg
Solistin:
Moura Lympany, Klavier
Walter Piston: Toccata
Serge Rachmaninoff:
Erstes Klavierkonzert in
fis-moll
Ludwig van Beethoven:
Dritte Sinfonie in Es-dur,
op. 55, «Eroica»

1967

Konzerte der
Tonhalle-Gesellschaft

4. Orchesterkonzert
Dienstag, den 27. Juni 1967
Leitung: Wolfgang Sawallisch
Solist: Josef Suk, Violine
Wolfgang Amadeus Mozart:
«Neue Lambacher-Sinfonie»,
KV 45a
Antonin Dvorak:
Violinkonzert in a-moll, op. 53
Igor Strawinsky: Sinfonie in C

5. Orchesterkonzert
Dienstag, den 4. Juli 1967
Leitung: Rudolf Kempe
Solisten: Trio di Trieste
Ludwig van Beethoven:
Tripelkonzert in C-dur, op. 56
Richard Strauss:
Eine Alpensinfonie, op. 64

Vorverkaufsstellen:
Tonhallekasse, Tug & Co. Limmatquai
Pianohaus Jecklin, Pfauen
Reisebüro Kuoni AG, Bahnhofplatz

Preise der Einzelkarten
an für die fünf Orchesterkonzerte Fr. 9.–
bis 24.–
b) für den Liederabend Fr. 4.50 bis 15.–
c) für den Kammermusikabend Fr. 4.40
bis 9.90

40

41

84

konrad wachsmann

bauen in unserer zeit

kunstgewerbemuseum zürich

ausstellung   24. mai bis 6. juli 1958
offen: montag 14-18 uhr
dienstag bis freitag 10-12, 14-18, 20-22 uhr
samstag und sonntag 10-12, 14-17 uhr
eintritt frei

müller-brockmann druck i.c. müller zürich

42

das freundliche Handzeichen

schützt vor Unfällen

43

Radfahrer-
Achtung.
Achtung-
Radfahrer

44

Überholen…?
Im Zweifel nie!

45

Rücksicht=Sicherheit

46

Automobil—Club der Schweiz

schützt das Kind!

Dick Elffers

Dick Elffers est plus qu'un dessinateur, ce qui veut dire qu'il ne se limite pas à une expression esthétique en soi, mais qu'il cherche à soumettre cette esthétique à une fonction. La structure et l'ordonnance doivent être adaptées à chaque fonction particulière.

Ce point de départ essentiel est constant, quel que soit le champ d'activité du créateur: le dessin donne sa signification au texte, le plan d'une exposition soutient l'expression de ce qui est exposé, la lisibilité rend le message d'une affiche plus perceptible.

Apparamment discrète, la norme esthétique joue un rôle définitif dans la création. L'élément esthétique, par exemple, de la typographie d'un texte doit être entièrement un problème d'ordonnance, étant lui-même fonction de cette ordonnance. La beauté typographique d'un texte peut, en éliminant les éléments qui sont subordonnés à l'esthétique, favoriser la lisibilité, comme le fait la clarté fonctionnelle de certains caractères typographiques.

L'introduction de la couleur dans une exposition peut en soutenir le

Dick Elffers is more than just a draftsman. That is to say, he does not limit himself to the production of beautiful designs for their own sake, but also seeks to subject each piece of styling to a function. Structure and order must be adapted to each particular function.

This basic point of origine is constant, irrespective of the field of activity in which a creative artist works. An illustration adds significance to a text, an exhibition design enhances the expression of that which is exhibited and legibility renders the message of a poster more intelligible.

Although not superficially obvious, aesthetic standards play a definitive role in creative work. The visual appearance of the typography in a text, for example, should be exclusively a problem of order, since it is itself a function of that order. The typographical beauty of a text may be given improved legibility by eliminating those elements that are subordinate to visual appearance, as is the case with the functional clarity of certain typographical characters.

The introduction of color into a

Dick Elffers ist nicht nur Zeichner, d.h. er gibt sich nicht mit der bloßen Schönheit eines Designs zufrieden, sondern ist bestrebt, jede seiner Kreationen einer Funktion zu unterordnen. Struktur und Form müssen stets einer jeweils gegebenen Funktion dienen. Dieser Ausgangspunkt ändert sich nicht, so unterschiedlich die Gebiete, auf denen der schöpferische Künstler arbeitet, auch sein mögen. Eine Illustration kann die Aussage eines Textes bedeutungsvoller machen, das Arrangement einer Ausstellung, den Ausdruck dessen, was ausgestellt ist, intensivieren, die gesteigerte Leserlichkeit, die Botschaft eines Plakates wirksamer «verkaufen».

Obschon nicht auf den ersten Blick erkennbar, spielen ästhetische Normen im kreativen Prozeß eine entscheidende Rolle. So sollte z.B. das ästhetische Element der Typographie eines Textes ausschließlich eine Frage der richtigen Anordnung sein, da es seinerseits Funktion dieser Anordnung ist derjenigen Elemente durch Eliminierung, die der Ästhetik dienen. Die typographische Schönheit eines Textes kann seine Leserlich-

plan et en faire un tout attractif et plaisant. Mais une norme esthétique s'impose aussi avec force par sa valeur intrinsèque sans avoir, de ce fait, une signification évidente. Dans ce cas, le dessin n'a pas de fonction; les initiales ornées des manuscrits médiévaux en sont un exemple.

Les normes esthétiques jouent un rôle important dans le développement fonctionnel du dessin, rencontrant par là les conventions que l'histoire a établies. Le dessin a connu un développement semblable à celui de l'architecture: partant d'une simple unité d'habitation, elle est arrivée aujourd'hui à une structure complexe qui nécessite une esthétique fonctionnelle. La part, non évidente à première vue, que joue l'esthétique dans le dessin pousse le créateur à inventer celle qui lui est propre.

Ce qui est le plus important, c'est d'adapter cette esthétique à une fonction définie. Pour un créateur comme Dick Elffers, l'esthétique est un langage personnel qui lui permet de s'exprimer dans n'importe quel domaine de la création. La personnalité du dessinateur se manifeste par son langage propre appliqué à une fonction, langage qu'il a défini lui-même. Ce qui, par

conséquent, n'en fait pas un disciple, son attitude étant différente de celle du peintre. Cependant, on peut la comparer à celle des peintres en face de la perspective: non pas une suggestion de la troisième dimension, mais l'énoncé d'un système spatial.

display may enhance the design and lead to an attractive, pleasing entity. But aesthetic standards may also exert an intrinsically powerful effect without thereby assuming any evident significance. In this case the design is not functional. An example is provided by the illuminated initials of medieval manuscripts.

Aesthetic standards play an important part in the functional development of a design, where they act in conjunction with conventions established by history. Designing has evolved in lines similar to architecture. Starting from the simple dwelling unit, architecture is today concerned with complex structures demanding functional styling. The part played by styling in design, though it may not be obvious at first sight, impels the creative artist to produce work that is typically his own.

The most important thing is to adapt to a defined function. For a creative artist like Dick Elffers visual styling is a personal language that bles him to express himself irrespective of the creative field involved. The personality of a designer is shown by the way he applies his own language, defined by himself, to a given function. This does not mean that his work must be derivative, for his attitude is different from that of a painter. However, it may be compared to that of a painter toward perspective —it is not merely a method of suggesting the third dimension but the anunciation of a spatial system. This does not of course mean that

keit begünstigen, wie es durch die funktionelle Deutlichkeit bestimmter typographischer Buchstaben geschieht.

Das Hineinbringen von Farbe in eine Ausstellung kann deren Absicht und Anordnung deutlicher und aus ihr eine attraktive und gefällige Einheit machen. Aber eine ästhetische Norm vermag durch ihren inneren Wert gewaltsam aufzudrängen, ohne dadurch schon eine augenscheinliche Bedeutung zu erlangen. In diesem Falle übt das Design keine Funktion aus (z.B. verzierte Initialen mittelalterlicher Texte).

Ästhetische Normen spielen in der funktionellen Entwicklung des Designs eine wichtige Rolle, wobei sie mit den von der Geschichte herausgebildeten Konventionen zusammentreffen. Als kreative Gattung hat das Design eine Entwicklung durchlaufen, die derjenigen der Architektur ähnelt. Ausgehend von einer einfachen Wohneinheit, ist sie heute mit komplexen Strukturen befaßt, die eine funktionelle Ästhetik verlangen. Die zunächst nicht ohne weiteres erkennbare Bedeutung, welche die Ästhetik im graphischen Design spielt, drängt — mag sie auch zunächst nicht ohne weiteres erkennbar sein — zu unverwechselbar eigenständiger Kreativität. Das Wichtigste ist, diese Ästhetik einer bestimmten Funktion anzupassen. Für einen Künstler wie Dick Elffers ist die Ästhetik eine persönliche Ausdruckweise, die ihm erlaubt, sich auf jedem Gebiet der künstlerischen Gestaltung auszudrücken. Die Persönlichkeit des Graphikers manifestiert sich in der Art, wie er seine von ihm selbst definierte Ausdrucksweise auf eine Funktion anwendet. Daraus folgt jedoch nicht, daß seine Arbeit eklektisch sein muß, denn seine Geisteshaltung unterscheidet sich von derjenigen eines Malers. Dennoch läßt sie sich mit der Einstellung der Maler zur Perspektive vergleichen: geht es ihnen doch weniger um

Dick Elffers

Cela n'exclut pas, bien sûr, la sensibilité de l'artiste et sa difficulté à trouver un langage personnel. C'est cette difficulté qui permet au créateur de connaître plus complètement les possibilités de son langage propre et, par conséquent, d'aboutir à une liberté totale d'expression.

artistic sensitivity is excluded or that there is no difficulty about finding a personal language. But it is this difficulty that permits a creative artist to be more completely aware of the possibilities of his own language and by consequence to attain total liberty of expression in the final result.

Vortäuschung der dritten Dimension als um den Ausdruck eines räumlichen Systems. Damit soll selbstverständlich weder die Bedeutung der künstlerischen Sensibilität geschmälert noch die Schwierigkeit, eine persönliche Ausdrucksweise zu finden, in Abrede gestellt werden.

1910   Né à Rotterdam.
1929–1933   Etudie la peinture et le graphisme à l'Académie des Beaux-Arts de Rotterdam.
1933–1940   Peint et crée des œuvres graphiques.
1940–1945   Interrompu dans son activité par la Seconde Guerre mondiale.
1945   S'installe à Amsterdam.

1910   Born in Rotterdam.
1929-33   Studied painting and graphics at the Rotterdam Academy of Arts.
1933-40   Painted and created graphic works.
1940-45   Activities interrupted by World War II.
1945   Established himself in Amsterdam.

1910   In Rotterdam geboren.
1929-33   Studierte Malerei und Graphik an der Akademie der Künste in Rotterdam.
1933-40   Malte und führte graphische Arbeiten aus.
1940-45   Unterbrechung der künstlerischen Tätigkeit durch den Zweiten Weltkrieg.
1945   Ließ sich in Amsterdam nieder.

Actuellement, son activité se manifeste dans les domaines de la peinture, du graphisme et de l'art monumental. Il est créateur attitré du «Rijksmuseum» à Amsterdam, pour la conception des expositions.

At the present time he works in the fields of painting, graphics, and monumental art. He is an exhibition designer by appointment to the Amsterdam Rijksmuseum.

Zur Zeit ist er als Maler, Graphiker und Designer und zugleich als Ausstellungsgestalter für das «Rijksmuseum» in Amsterdam tätig.

Dick Elffers

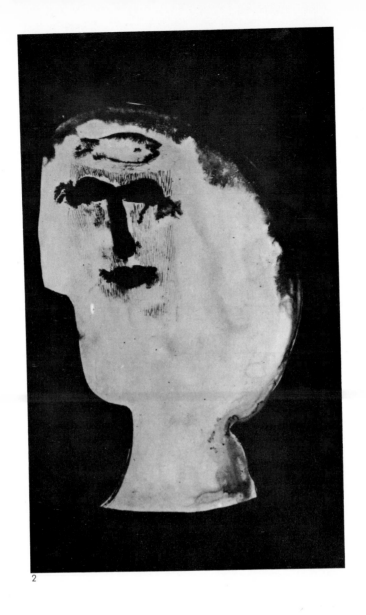

2

3

4

5

Holland
festival

Amsterdam
Den Haag

15
juni
15
juli
1959

fly there
by
K L M

filmweek
Arnhem

Holland festival

19
-
24
juni
1959

FILM

internationale
filmweek
Arnhem
juni 19-24-'59

7

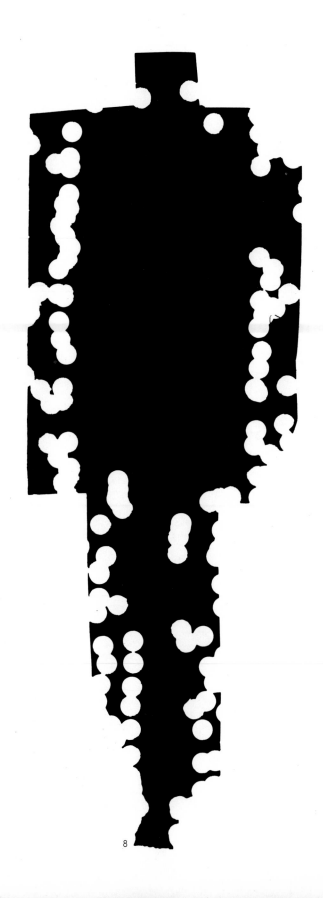

8

11

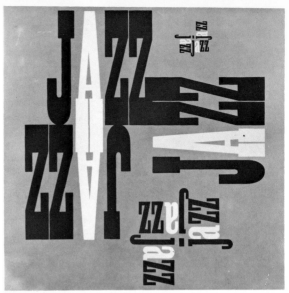

12

13

14

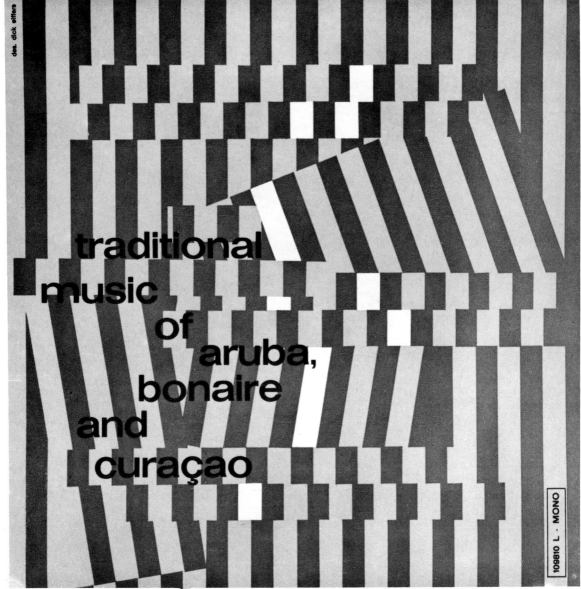

des. dick elffers

traditional music of aruba, bonaire and curaçao

109810 L - MONO

15

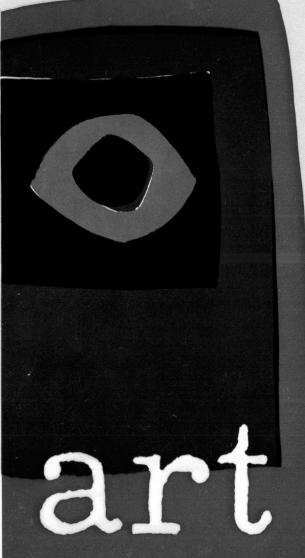

april 21 - october 21

seattle, wash., u.s.a. 1962

art

since 1950

seattle world's fair

16

5 mei
maak er een feest van

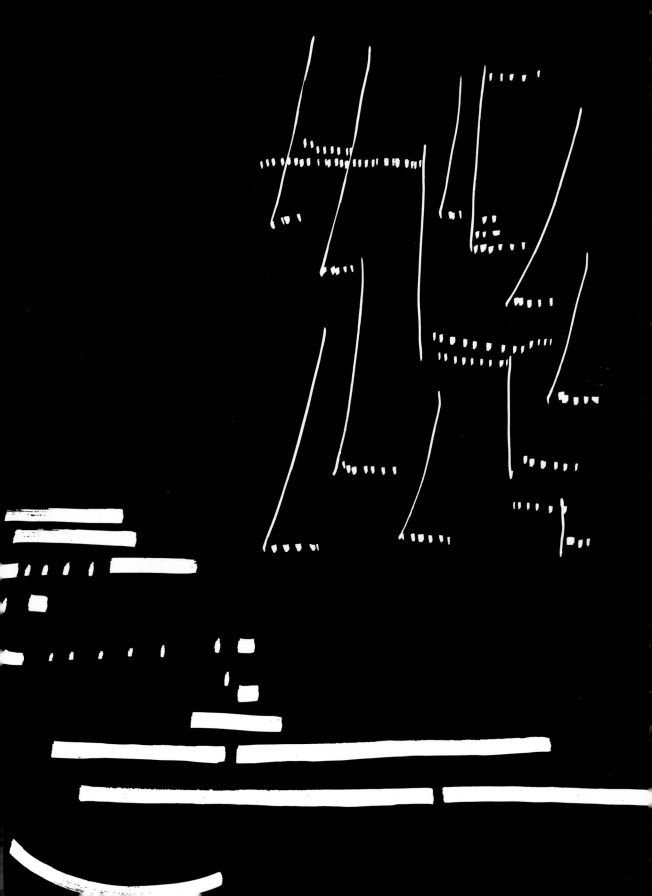

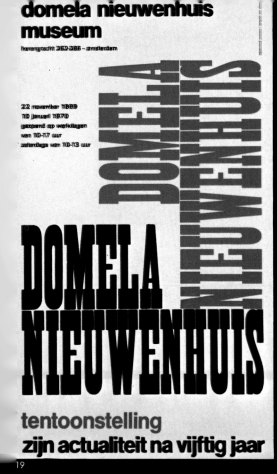

19

20

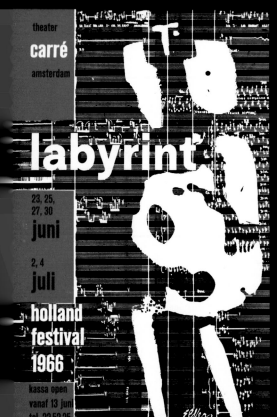

amsterdam   den haag   rotterdam

15 juni

9 juli

holland
festival '69

24

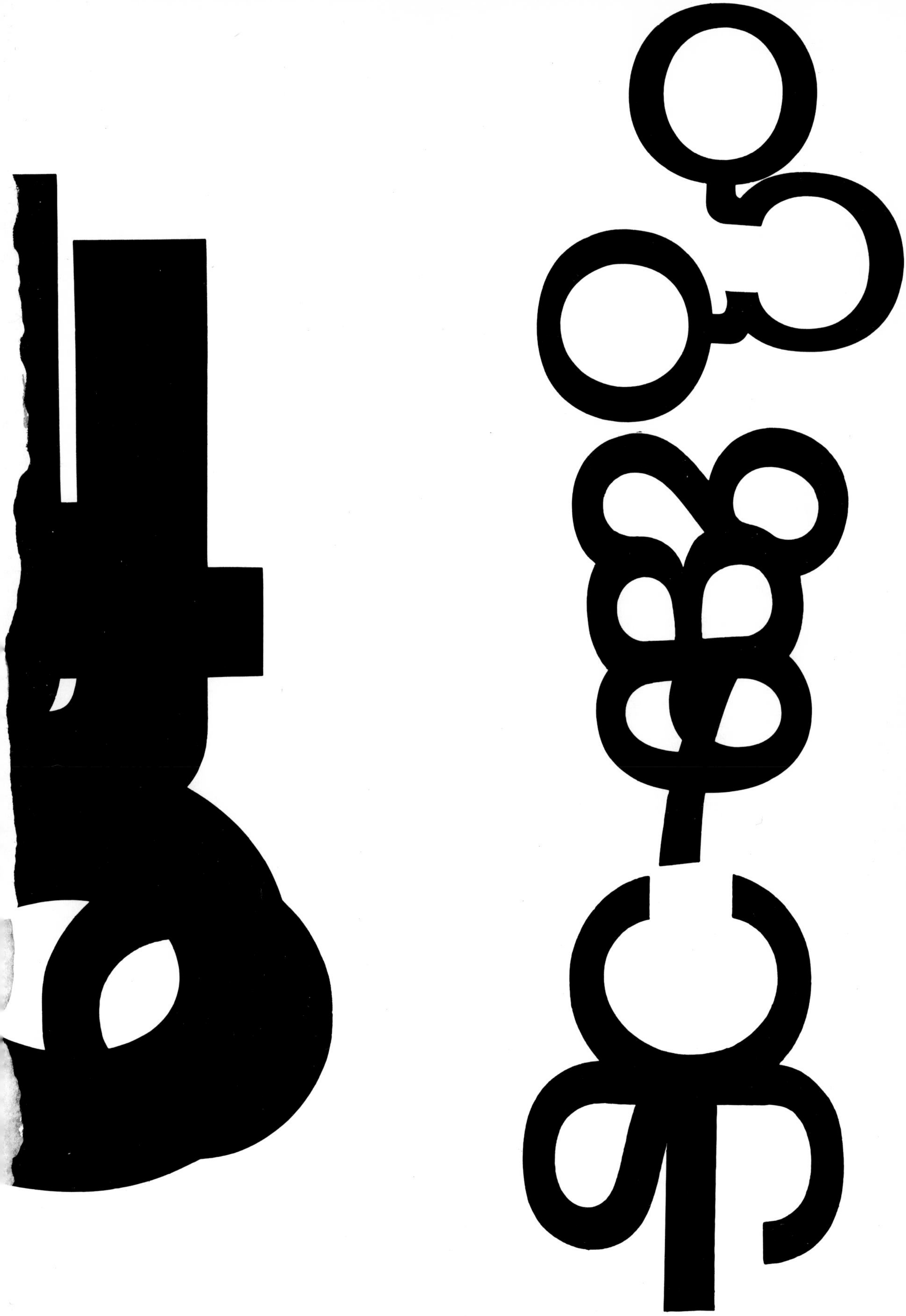

25

26

27

28

Cet ouvrage a été achevé d'imprimer en mars 1971 par Bijutsu Shuppan-sha, Tokyo. La photocomposition a été confiée à la Maison Stauffer & Cie, Bâle (Suisse).
La maquette a été réalisée par Gan Hosoya.

Imprimé et relié en Japon

This book was printed by Bijutsu Shuppan-sha, Tokyo. Photocomposition by Stauffer & Co., Basle (Switzerland). The lay-out was designed by Gan Hosoya.

Printed and bound in Japan

Satz: Stauffer & Co., Basel (Schweiz).
Druck: Bijutsu Shuppan-sha, Tokio.
Gestaltung: Gan Hosoya.

Printed and bound in Japan